SOLVED

"Sir" Adam Kleinberg
and Adam "The Phantom" Nudelman

ECW Press

Published by ECW Press
2120 Queen Street East, Suite 200, Toronto, Ontario, Canada M4E 1E2

LIBRARY AND ARCHIVES CANADA CATALOGUING IN PUBLICATION

Kleinberg, Adam
Mysteries of wrestling: solved / Adam Kleinberg and Adam Nudelman.

ISBN 1-55022-685-1

1. Wrestling. I. Nudelman, Adam II. Title.

GV1195.K54 2005   796.812   C204–907054–1

Editor for the press: Michael Holmes
Typesetting: Mary Bowness
Front cover photos: Marco Shark, Mark Fisette, Mike Lano, Larry Plitnick
Back cover photos: Mike Lano, Larry Plitnick
Spine photo: Gordon Tepper
Printing: Printcrafters

This book is set in Boton, Imago and Metaphor

The publication of *Mysteries of Wrestling: Solved* has been generously supportedby the Ontario Arts Council, and the Government of Canada through the Book Publishing Industry Development Program. We acknowledge the support of the Canada Council for the Arts for our publishing program. Canadä

DISTRIBUTION

Canada: Jaguar Book Group, 100 Armstrong Ave., Georgetown, ON L7G 5S4

United States: Independent Publishers Group, 814 North Franklin Street, Chicago, Illinois 60610

PRINTED AND BOUND IN CANADA

ECW PRESS
ecwpress.com

Contents

PHOTO CREDITS

ACKNOWLEDGEMENTS

"Sir Adam" Kleinberg would like to thank the following people:

My beautiful wife Tracy, for all of her help in transcribing interviews, editing my verbosity and thinking up the title. You are my inspiration and have helped me achieve all of my dreams. I love you, forevermore.

My daughter Maya, whose smile has forever brightened my days.

My dad, for helping us get our show off the ground and for taking me to all those wrestling matches when I was a kid.

My mom, for buying me stuff like the Hulk Hogan foam finger when my dad thought it was too expensive and for her undying confidence in me.

My sisters, who unselfishly did things like make banners and received nothing more than figure four leg locks in return.

My friend Adam, for making this the most fun adventure in the world.

Lauren and Dennis for all your help and for not forbidding your daughter from marrying someone who is obsessed with wrestling.

Adam "Phantom" Nudelman would like to thank the following people:

My gorgeous wife, Glenne, for changing my life and filling it with joy. For being there for me during the creation of this book. You are my everything, I love you.

My baby girl Nicole for giving my life purpose

My parents for supporting me throughout my life, no matter what.

My brother Dave, for all the two out of three falls death matches we wrestled during our youth.

Larry and Janice, thanks for the pictures and the encouragement.

The authors would like to thank the following people:

Jack David and everyone at ECW Press. Eric Britton for encouraging us to be ourselves. The Iron Sheik for always being there for us when we didn't have a guest. Howard Stern, Opie & Anthony and Ron & Fez for making us strive to put on a great radio program. John Arezzi, Jody McDonald and Rich Mancuso for paving the way. Most importantly, we want to thank each and every wrestler who has ever appeared on GIR Radio and was interviewed for this book. And especially our listeners; without them, we wouldn't have been able to do what we've done.

The authors would also like to tell "The Matador" Tito Santana and "Captain" Mike Rotunda to go to hell for their refusal to be interviewed for this book. *Arriba!*

FOREWORD

It's 1990 and the two of us are fifteen year old kids listening to John Arezzi's weekly wrestling radio show on WGBB in New York. Sure, we could barely get the signal most days, and Arezzi, although ground-breaking, was not exactly the most riveting talk show host on the airwaves. But for us, it was the only gateway we knew, our only access to the mysteries of pro wrestling.

Phantom offering Sir Adam some constructive criticism

That is, until the fateful day when we realized that his show just wasn't giving us the answers we wanted. We spoke to other wrestling fans we knew and they all agreed with us, but unfortunately, it was the only show of its kind around. So we figured, if wrestlers would talk to Arezzi, why wouldn't they talk to us? We needed to start our own radio show so we could finally get answers to all of our questions. Not just whether the sleeperhold really works (see chapter 11), but just what the hell is that blotch on Dusty Rhodes' stomach (see chapter 8)?

We're both thirty now, which means we've spent the better part of the next two decades trying to understand the mysteries of wrestling. The first thing we did was to learn about the inner workings of the business and to do that we spent hours on the phone with wrestling journalists like "Stately" Wayne Manor and wrestlers such as the late "Boston Bad Boy" Tony Rumble. By 1991, we were ready to hit the airwaves on our local high school radio station, WKWZ.

Now, if you've ever listened to high school radio, you know it's a painful combination of shout-outs and teenage angst. But *Get in the Ring*, which soon became affectionately known as *GIR Radio*, was different. In fact, it was emphatically praised by the faculty members overseeing the station and people started to take notice as we soon had listeners from all over Long Island, something previously unheard of for a high school radio show.

We took time off to study communication in college and started up again on WGBB in 1996. We later moved on to a larger station, WLIE, but unfortunately, our dreams of being discovered and eventually syndicated have never progressed passed that, the dream stage. However, through the power of the Internet, we have been able to amass a grass roots cult following all around the world and that is something that has made spending half our lives working on a project with no financial reward worth our while. Along the way, we've been able to find many of the answers we were looking for and learned that some mysteries can't be solved — they just lead to more questions. In fact, *GIR Radio* has been first on the scene when it comes to covering some of the bigger stories in wrestling since the mid 90s. We had the first interview with Bret Hart following the legendary Montreal incident, and you'll read about it in Chapter 9. And as you'll discover in Chapter 5, *GIR Radio* was on the scene to find out just why Steve Austin refused to work with Jeff Jarrett.

Just remember, while we're both brutally honest in this book, the two of us don't always see eye to eye. In fact, on the air we're usually lambasting each other from start to finish. But the answer to the first mystery in this book is that we're just two wrestling fans who managed to find out the answers to most of our questions in a unique way. So for much of this book we'll write in this narrative style, but at times our individual radio characters will have to speak out.

PHANTOM

Thank God I'm able to separate my thoughts from Sir Adam's. I can't be expected to go along with whatever he says, like that time he pegged Val Venis as being the next WWE world champion.

SIR ADAM

This coming from the man who in 1996 said that Booker T was the weak link in Harlem Heat.

Just another day at the GIR office

PHANTOM

Who knew he could do the spinarooni back then?

And of course, a book about wrestling would not be complete without comments from wrestlers themselves. Inside you'll find new interviews with wrestling's finest from the past and present, specifically conducted for this book. Additionally, we searched our radio archives and each chapter features special guest appearances — from Terry Funk to Hulk Hogan to The Rock. So start reading — so we can get on with our lives.

Chapter 1

Was There Really a Cannibal in Wrestling?

Kevin Sullivan: The original Sheik was a dear friend of mine and he was the Sheik twenty-four hours a day. I mean his credit card said "A. Sheik." He didn't speak and that's why I think he was successful for so long.

A professional wrestling match comes down to two, three or four athletes, all competing to win. And athletes, like others from all walks of life, come in different shapes and sizes. However, wrestling throws an interesting factor into the mix, something no other "sport" can offer— the gimmick. While you've never seen a baseball player wearing a cape or a hockey player dressed up like a member of KISS, over the years there have been wrestlers who impersonated everything from clowns to Elvis. And some of the characters that these wrestlers portrayed have been so out there that most people are left walking away wondering what these guys are really like outside of the ring.

Bobby "the Brain" Heenan: Hmmm. Well, let me put it this way. I wouldn't want none of them to do my taxes, or to give me a vasectomy or circumcision. Would you?

"The Brain" has a point. But what we've discovered is that the further off the beaten path a wrestler appears on TV, the more interested wrestling fans become in learning what they're like outside of the ring. And the most intriguing of the gimmick wrestlers are the group who portrayed savages, lunatics and cannibals. In researching this book, we spoke with everyone from Kamala to the Missing Link, and the one thing they all agreed upon is that not speaking all of those years was tough on them. They are a unique group, and to understand their mindset, you have to speak with the most legendary gimmick wrestler of all time, George "the Animal" Steele.

George "the Animal" Steele: There's a lot of history behind George "the Animal" Steele that people don't understand — because they're young and George was around a long time. When I first went to New York in the WWWF, in about 1967, I had no manager. I did all my own talking. And I was pretty articulate, believe it or not.

Being a full-time Phys Ed. teacher in his home state of Michigan, George only wrestled part time for most of his career. Basically, wrestling was his summer job. Nonetheless, his legacy of being a green-tongued animal that couldn't speak started, oddly enough, while he was doing a promo.

George "the Animal" Steele: I'm talking, the Grand Wizard's talking, and he looked at me. He shut the mic off; he said, "Let's do that again, you're making too much sense for an animal." Well, it kind of pissed me off. So I figured I'll show them. So the cameras come back on, we're doing the interview, and the mic comes to me and I went, "Uhhh, uhhh." And he said, "That's it. That's what I want." I went, "Oh crap." I liked doing interviews.

SIR ADAM

Maybe if I start calling Phantom an animal he'll finally stop talking so much.

PHANTOM

So what do I have to call you to shut your fancy transplanted British face? You know, I can't imagine not being able to talk. Actually, I can't even imagine having a gimmick. Thank God we don't have to do that.

SIR ADAM

Right, like your drivers license says The Phantom and I really come from Hoggarth, England.

PHANTOM

You don't?

After speaking with George and others, we realized that when a wrestler's character doesn't speak, the fans really want to know more. They want to know what the "animal" is really like, and how much of what they see on television is just an act. The seemingly simple task of appearing mute creates a certain mystique that is not obtainable in any other way. The "Russian Bear" Ivan Koloff spent the early part of his career remaining silent and summed it up best.

Ivan Koloff: They see this big, impressive guy beating everyone up but not really saying much. And when he did say things it was just short, growly and mean. They wanted to know you, but you weren't letting them. To me I think it added to it.

Another guy who didn't speak more than an occasional grunt and groan was Ivan's "nephew," the "Russian Nightmare" Nikita Koloff. The product of the Cold War era, Nikita was essentially wrestling's equivalent of the Drago character in *Rocky IV*. He was big, strong, scary and Russian — or so we thought.

SIR ADAM

We had Nikita on the show in 1998 and it was really cool — he was always one of our idols. Which was why we were really excited when he told us he would be in New York in a few weeks and that he would love to get together for dinner.

PHANTOM

I couldn't wait to eat some high-class Russian food. I was so excited that I was this close to shaving my head and growing a goatee just to fit in. Well, it's a good thing that I didn't because we ate at Outback Steakhouse and he looked more like a high school gym teacher on parent night. Clean shaven and all decked out in a pastel-colored polo shirt and khakis.

SIR ADAM

We had no idea he was bringing his wife. If we had, we probably would have brought dates. Nikita and his wife seemed a little surprised to see two twenty-four year old guys waiting for them, but we went to the restaurant anyway. And I was more than a little surprised that Nikita now had a full head of hair. Was this really Nikita and why was he so excited to go the Outback Steakhouse?

PHANTOM

Mrs. Koloff thought we were gay. What an idiot. Why would she presume we would bring dates to meet Nikita Koloff? Unlike her, it's not every girl's dream to meet the Russian Nightmare. The whole dinner I couldn't stop thinking that while he looked like he could be Nikita's cousin or uncle, there was no way the Soviet bastard I saw on TV could be so cordial. What a gentleman. Or so we thought.

SIR ADAM

Dinner was cool and Nikita told us how he met his wife, that they thought we were gay for not bringing dates and that he fixed up Road Warrior Animal with his wife. And while I must admit that the thought of Road Warrior Animal in his Zubaz pants, stupid Mohawk and face paint sitting in a fancy restaurant on a double date with our new best friends kept my interest for a few minutes, mostly, I was just wondering what happened to Nikita's Russian accent.

Actually, he wasn't really Russian. He spoke perfect English — he originally hails from Minnesota. In fact, you'd be surprised how many "Russian" wrestlers weren't really Russian at all. Real life events often have a way of carrying over into wrestling storylines and characters, and the Cold War was no different. It made for the perfect wrestling heel, the evil Soviet. Ivan Koloff? He's the product of a French family who lived in Canada, but would you have ever been afraid of the French-Canadian Bear? Perhaps what we find even stranger is that many of these guys were actually American. Remember Boris Zukhov? You know, the Russian guy with the really big head. Well, his real name is Jim Nelson and he lives in North Carolina. You can't get any more American than that. Krusher Khrushchev? Sorry, but he's from Minnesota, too. What it all adds up to is that the "evil foreigner" is just another gimmick, less obvious than the savage who doesn't talk, but a gimmick nonetheless.

PHANTOM

Can we get back to the story? We're just getting to the good part.

SIR ADAM

We were wrapping up and the most awkward moment came when the check arrived.

PHANTOM

Keep in mind that I had just gotten through explaining how I was living in my parents' house and trying to get a career started after college and was making no money and Sir Adam had told Nikita that he was in law school and also broke.

SIR ADAM

It was quiet and I thought we were supposed to offer to pay, but I didn't think he'd take us up on it. We were two poor kids and he was the former NWA U.S. Champion. Anyway, I offered and Nikita accepted. We were stunned. He and his wife both had shrimp and steak and it cost a fortune.

Ivan Koloff: Nikita always ate good.

Getting to the bottom of the Outback Steakhouse controversy with Ivan Koloff

PHANTOM

I kept waiting for him to say "Just kidding" or "Got ya!", but he stayed silent. As silent as he was when he portrayed the 'Russian Nightmare.' Sir Adam and I got our cash together.

George "the Animal" Steele: Everybody knew I could talk. Hell, they couldn't shut me up.

Actually, not everyone knew that. Often, when a young wrestler would come into the locker room and find out he was wrestling George "the Animal" Steele, it would be a very difficult experience.

George "the Animal" Steele: I would just look at them and stare. I would work them. In other words, if somebody comes in, they'd never come over to me, they'd stand in the corner and kind of look at me. And I would go very quiet. All the other boys would be laughing. I'd just walk over and act like I was going to smell 'em. They didn't know what I was going to do.

I've got him right where I want him. 'Cause I'm the animal, I want them to show fear and, their fear, it's there, it's real. They don't know what they're going to do. I was pretty good at what I did and I could make them do what I wanted them to do in a lot of cases.

You see, George didn't like to talk over a match with anyone and many other gimmick wrestlers were the same way. When they had an opportunity to have a guy they were working with think that they were real-life wildmen, they seized it. Their thinking was that if their opponent didn't know what was going to happen in the ring, it only added to the realism of the match. In fact, to a certain extent, George even used these types of mind games with guys who were more than just nervous rookies looking for a payday. One name that comes to mind is Randy "Macho Man" Savage.

George "the Animal" Steele: The first time I'm gonna wrestle with him, after I chased Liz a couple of times, we're on a *Saturday Night Main Event*, and he comes in with like a little book of a whole match written out. First of all, I'll be honest with you, I didn't like it. Because I'd been around at that point for twenty-five, thirty years. And here's some young punk coming in and telling me what we're gonna do. Instead of asking me, telling me. So I look at him like "Yeah, okay." I read the whole thing and, as I read it, I start taking the pages, wrinkling them up and throwing [them] in the trashcan, just staring at him. And he's getting hot.

The thing with Randy was everything we did was fairly real 'cause he really loved Elizabeth. He was really jealous. It was the real deal . . . Anytime I would look at Elizabeth, even when he was in the locker room, he'd get hot . . . I said, "Remember, I've gotta heck of a run with some of these young broads around here." Which I really didn't, but he didn't know. Fire was coming out of his nose. I'd go out to the ring and he'd come out all fired up, which was what I wanted.

> Wrestling is a strange business. Most times, a promoter takes one look at you and decides whether you're going to wear a three-piece suit or a chicken suit to the ring. These decisions can affect a wrestler's entire professional career. Just picture for a minute Kamala as a member of the Four Horseman, or William Regal as one of the Moondogs. It just doesn't seem right, does it? So we wanted to know where the strangest and one of the most talked about gimmicks of all time started. We set off to find Doink the Clown, who to us always appeared to be an evil, drunken, well . . . clown.

SIR ADAM

> We figured where better to find a drunken clown than at the circus. So we got a bottle of Tequila and hit the big top. We didn't find Doink, but I nearly died when Phantom threw up on a four year old girl sitting in front of us.

PHANTOM

Don't ever drink six shots of tequila and get too close to the elephants.

Well that didn't work. But we got a lead and were able to find Matt Borne, the original "Doink the Clown," alive and well in the Pacific Northwest. We found out that Matt's parents divorced when he was about ten years old and he went to live with his dad. Which would be a somewhat normal occurrence, except that Matt's dad was "Tough" Tony Borne, a legendary wrestler

Matt Borne as Doink the Clown

in the Pacific Northwest. So Matt spent most of his childhood on the road, essentially growing up in the dressing room around a bunch of wrestlers.

Matt "Doink the Clown" Borne: Vince McMahon and I were sitting there talking about my upbringing in the business, and I told him about how I grew up in the dressing room and Lonny Mayne, he was Moondog Mayne, him and my dad we're pretty tight and he was just a ribber from hell. He was always ribbing the other guys, locking their boots up. In high school gyms they would find these loose locks and lock their boots together. So I thought that was pretty funny — here's this grown man, but he was always drunk. I don't think he could work if he wasn't drunk. Here I was around this atmosphere all the time and I kind of like thought the sun rose and set in Lonny's butt. So when I was sitting there talking to Vince about all this, that's, I think, what sparked the Doink character. At first it threw me for a loop, because all these years I tried to portray myself as a tough guy and here's Vince wanting to make a clown out of me.

Who knew there was so much meaning behind the character? We always just thought he was a drunken clown.

Matt "Doink the Clown" Borne: I wasn't supposed to be a drunk clown, but just the fact that I grew up around this horseplay all the time, I think that sparked him.

Gimmicks come from all sorts of places. Some like Matt's are based on fun times and others are based on the deepest and darkest places of a person's soul. While no one will ever forget how Jake Roberts would walk to the ring carrying a large burlap sack containing his pet python Damien, a tactic he regularly employed to intimidate his opponents, the truth is the real key to Jake the Snake's success was the character's dark and complex mental state. Jake was the ultimate thinker and he played mind games with everyone he encountered.

Jake "the Snake" Roberts: Jake "the Snake" Roberts was created due to a misguided, misplaced, abused childhood, if you will. And I'm not blaming anybody, that's what I got. And that was my cards, not my crime, okay?

SIR ADAM

Maybe we should move on.

PHANTOM

Let's keep trying. This is a long distance call to England.

Jake "the Snake" Roberts: The Snake was basically the way I lived. I was very quiet, alone. I was always a mystery. "What's going on in his mind and where is he coming from?" Because they didn't know what had happened to me and the last damn thing I wanted to do was tell them . . . The Snake was the character, but Jake was the guy that came along and protected that little kid that got lost.

Moving on to some one a little saner, Kamala . . . Yes, Kamala. Even though he always needed to be accompanied to the ring by both a manager and a safari tour guide who wore a mask, Jim Harris is one of the nicest guys we've ever come across in the wrestling business. So how did Jim Harris turn into Kamala, the Ugandan Giant?

Kamala "the Ugandan Giant": I used to live in Kenya . . . and I saw a lot of that stuff over there and I brought a lot of stuff back. Jerry Lawler gave me the name Kimala, K-I-M-A-L-A. But then I later changed it because a guy named the great Mephisto, Frankie Cain, had already come up with the gimmick when I was living in Africa. But, Lawler, I got to give it to him, he helped me out a lot.

Anyone need a hug?

As scary as Kamala can look and act, he is easily the most misunderstood of the gimmick wrestlers. These days, he works as a truck driver, wrestles part-time, has a family, and resides in Texas. For him, the most fun part of wrestling was portraying a character so unlike who he is in his day-to-day life.

Kamala "the Ugandan Giant": I'm just an actor playing a part. I think I'm a real cool guy and everybody seems to like me. I get along with everybody in wrestling, but I like playing the part. I love playing the part. I like seeing the expression on people's faces and I like the crowd reaction. You know, when I come out, it just makes me connect to the part even more.

SIR ADAM

I went backstage at an indy show once where a lot of stars from the '80s and '90s were performing. The Road Warriors, Brutus Beefcake, Tatanka, Stan Hansen. The late Road Warrior Hawk asked me to be Kamala's "bodyguard" and take him to the autograph table. I'm only about 5'6" so as you can imagine, Kamala found this quite amusing. Anyway, even though I got to meet many of my childhood heroes that day, I walked away most surprised by how Kamala was just a guy who enjoyed being part of the show and, most of all, being in front of the fans. You could just see on his face how much he enjoyed the spectacle of it all and the camaraderie in the locker room. In a strange way, I was kind of disappointed that he was as nice as he was. I was expecting a savage and I got a teddy bear.

PHANTOM

That last line was so gay. I can't believe you wrote that.

For most wrestlers, a gimmick is an opportunity to live out an alter ego. A license to create a persona that they could never let loose in everyday society. And generally this is a positive experience.

Baron Von Raschke: It was a great release. You know, Baron, he was, is and always will be my alter ego. I couldn't live like that twenty-four hours a day, but he could say what he wanted to, and do what he wanted to. I'm a much quieter person. I like to be left alone and I don't need or seek the limelight. Whereas the Baron was a ham. He loved it.

Ivan Koloff: I felt that way also, in the sense that I think it gets a person out of their shell if you are kind of shy or introverted. It makes you become bolder.

Abdullah the Butcher (From a 5/02 *GIR Radio* Interview): Let's put it this way. When you first start going with a girl, when you start making love with her, I mean, you start raising a lot of hell. You start telling a lot of lies. You start screaming and hollering. And I'm the same way. When I get in the ring it's altogether different.

> Naturally, playing a character is often a life altering experience for a wrestler. And depending on the role portrayed and the individual's stake in the role, it can also become a negative. Jake Roberts had so many personal issues tied into his character that "the Snake" was, for him, a release of a different kind.

Jake "the Snake" Roberts: It hurt me and it's still hurting me. It's cheated me out of a lot of things in life, such as the ability to trust and love. I have a hard time with women because I was abused by a couple of them, you know. Even though I was very, very much in love with Cheryl, when it came to being really trustful and 100%, I had to push away because I was scared, because I knew the last time I did that I got hurt. It's a weird game, man, it wasn't fun. The Jake [character] came by to protect that little kid, made it safe for him, but Jake doesn't like that little kid because he's embarrassed by the bastard.

> Either way, it shows that wrestlers have to be able to hang up their masks and robes and check their characters at the door when they get home. They have to say "It's all in a day's work" in order to return to a sense of normalcy and go on with their everyday lives. How difficult that is depends on the individual and, more often than not, can be the difference between a happy life and a less fulfilling one.

Baron Von Raschke: It was easy. I just went back into my routine with my wife and children. Like I said, the Baron's a hard man. I couldn't live like that.

Kevin Sullivan: It's very hard, sometimes, not to let the gimmick take over. And I think one of the things I was always lucky with was really not letting the gimmick take me over, and kind of keeping my feet on the ground a little, was that I used my own name. You talk to guys that have a fictitious name and they'll talk about themselves in the third person.

"Gorgeous" Jimmy Garvin: I got so involved in the part that I actually started thinking and acting like this character to get prepared for the part. I played that part for twenty-three years and when I got home from work I was still Jimmy Garvin. Well, now I'm glad I got a break, because there is a little more to me than I've shown in those twenty-three years.

The anti-gimmick Bobby "the Brain" Heenan

While no one will disagree that it is difficult to successfully play a gimmick and get it over with the fans, there is a debate as to whether using a gimmick is taking the easy way out. One school of thought is that gimmicks are an attempt to either hide a wrestler's flaws or to get out of working hard in the ring.

Bobby "the Brain" Heenan: They think their gimmick will get over, but their work won't. There is no gimmick in this business that ever drew money as a world's champion. Dory Funk was not a gimmick. Terry Funk wasn't a gimmick. Jack Brisco wasn't a gimmick. Buddy Rogers wasn't a gimmick. Pat O'Connor, Dusty Rhodes . . . I mean, think about it, they were wrestlers. They didn't come from outer space or something. Believe me, those guys knew that. They thought they could walk around, shake their head, look at the clouds, kick you in the nuts, eat a turnbuckle . . . so they don't have to take bumps. They're lazy. That's what I think.

> Sorry Brain, but the gimmick wrestlers won't take this lying down.

George "the Animal" Steele: There are people that take gimmicks that don't know how to work. They hide themselves. But if you're working a gimmick and it's working with the crowd and the public, you're working harder than any wrestler in the ring.

Kamala "the Ugandan Giant": I'm not a scientific wrestler, but my gimmick doesn't call for that. I'm just a hit, kick, punch guy. But I could do stuff like, you know, Andre. I could do all that stuff, drop-kick . . . Well I used to be able to.

George "the Animal" Steele: Let's stop and think about it. [Mike Rotundo] never made any money as the wrestler from the University of Syracuse. They did the Varsity Club thing, it didn't mean nothing. It meant something when he got into his character I.R.S. Am I right or wrong? But he worked his tail off to make that work, if you remember. Gimmicks are not easy if they're done right.

> What it really comes down to is that there are only so many spots in wrestling and once you get one then you need to make the most of the opportunity. If a gimmick is that opportunity, you'd better work just as hard as the guy trying to get over on athletic ability.

Matt "Doink the Clown" Borne: You know what — even the Red Rooster — I could have gotten that rooster gimmick over. Terry Taylor hated it, but I mean, hell, if I would have hated Doink, if I would have went home and thought, Jesus, you know I'm gonna do this, but reluctantly, it wouldn't have flown. But I went home and, I'll be honest with you, I ate, drank and I just realized that if I can make this thing work well, it's Vince's idea and it's a new thing . . . it was going to get a push.

These days it seems as if gimmick wrestlers are being phased out of the product. There are fewer Hurricanes and more and more Randy Ortons. In fact, most wrestlers are simply using their real names or variations on them. This change in philosophy is not lost on the wrestlers who see that the business has changed drastically over the last twenty years. The gimmick wrestlers are sorely missed.

"Hacksaw" Jim Duggan: I think the old days of guys being carnival types are gone. Now you've got a lot of educated guys out there performing, and it shows.

PHANTOM

No matter what a veteran like Jim Duggan thinks, I miss the days where guys like Afa the Wild Samoan and Abdullah the Butcher reigned supreme. Where else can you see a guy take a bite out of a raw chicken on national television.

SIR ADAM

I think a lot of the gimmick wrestlers were fun to watch and they provided a nice compliment to the more technically-based matches. As a fan, I always like to see a little bit of everything on a show.

To this day, it's hard for us to believe that guys like the Koloffs weren't really Russian — they were that convincing. Nikita, the one who loves steak and shrimp, told us that in the late '80s, he was in character almost twenty four hours a day. In fact, when he would go to the gym, he would pretend that he couldn't speak any English and would stare at the other patrons as if they were his hated rival Dusty Rhodes. He wanted the fans to believe it that much, and they did.

Baron Von Raschke: I did a little bit of that. It's not an eight to five job you know. (Using Baron's voice) You choose to be a baron, you have to be a baron.

Kevin Sullivan: I was teamed up with Mark Lewin, the "Purple Haze," and we wore our robes just about anywhere so people would think . . . "maybe these guys are for real." In the car, driving to the town and coming back. Because that's one of the things I always thought about, when you saw a guy with great robes and this persona of being a big time spender and then you saw him leaving the building in shorts and flip-flops, well, it kinda broke the persona.

> We've found that some wrestlers really didn't want to go to such great lengths to hide their real personalities. For many, their profession is a passion; for all of them, however, it is still a job. And when they're not at work, most of them don't want to have to act like they're at work.

King Kong Bundy (From a 2/97 *GIR Radio* Interview): I'm always a gentleman outside the ring.

Viscera: I have had several people tell me that I am one of the nicest wrestlers they have ever met and that's because I just try to be a normal person. I've been a fan before and I know how it feels. I just try to treat people how I want to be treated. I've always been a regular person, that's the best way to do it. I mean, my character is so over the top, so evil looking. I'm such a big guy — it surprises people.

Joanie "Chyna" Laurer: I don't feel that I'm different from people, you know? I don't feel that way. I try to blend in. I used to see the fans as more of a nuisance, but now I value that they treat me differently.

Kevin Sullivan: I think in some ways the guys have it easier now because it's completely exposed and people know they're playing a persona. So they can check that persona in the arena when they leave, and pick it up when they come back.

Since the business has changed so much over the last twenty years, you no longer have to worry that when you try and talk to a guy like the Undertaker he'll want to bury you under thirty feet of dirt. It's a welcome change from the days when the Crusher would put out a cigar on your face. So if you see a gimmick wrestler in a restaurant, don't worry about him stabbing you with a fork. Go over and say "Hi." Just don't offer to pick up the check. He might take you up on it.

Chapter 2

Who's the Toughest Guy in Wrestling?

Bobby Eaton: I ain't got no stories about Meng.

Wrestling is a rough sport, you know it, we know it, but there are a select few sports entertainers who have earned the reputation of being legit tough guys. In the old days, these were guys who could handle themselves outside the ring to protect wrestling's reputation against those who tried to challenge the sport's legitimacy. Today, this same breed of fighter must also protect themselves from people trying to test them, as well as to maintain wrestling's status in a world that knows it is predetermined.

Sean Waltman: It's a tough business. Even though it's a work, if somebody has a legitimate reputation it adds to their mystique.

PHANTOM

This is a tough subject for me to talk about because I've never been a fighter. Yeah, I can talk a good game on the radio, but when it comes to hand-to-hand combat I try everything I can to stay away from it. One time in the infancy of *Get in the Ring* radio, back when Sir Adam and I were in high school, I made a crack about the football team. Something about them being "soft" and about how I couldn't believe they were actually getting laid. It was my jealousy talking, because *I* wasn't getting laid. *At all.* I never thought any of them would get wind of my comments, but they did, and for a period of about a month I had the entire football team looking to kick my ass. I couldn't sleep, and my only course of action was to hide out and carry a wrench to school. No kidding, at my suburban high school I was strapped like a prisoner at Riker's Island. Ultimately, nothing happened. After a while it just blew over, but the fear mixed with adrenaline, like any day could be my last, haunted me. What's really strange is that many wrestlers have told me that they love this feeling. They feed off of it because in the back of their minds they know that every time they step into a bar, there's a chance that the local tough guy will try to make a name for himself by beating up a professional wrestler. And they know that more often than not they can handle themselves in the face of that challenge.

Hacksaw Jim Duggan and Sir Adam, looking for a fight

Hacksaw Jim Duggan: The local tough guy, he might get into a fight once or twice a year, we're out there throwing punches and blocking punches every single night. I wouldn't try to do a plumber's job — and a plumber shouldn't try to do mine.

The question on every wrestling fan's mind has always been: who is the toughest wrestler, period? Not the guy who could best hold his own in the ring, but someone who could handle fifteen drunken sailors looking for trouble in a downtown bar. So, experts, how do you determine who it is?

Larry Zbyszko: Billy Robinson . . . and (Peter) Maivia got in a fight in Japan over who was the toughest. They are both drunk and they get in this fight, and Billy goes to hook some suplex move, a beautiful move, and he throws Maivia down on the ground and lands on top of him. Maivia, who was now under Robinson, started biting Billy in the chest through his shirt. Billy did the great wrestling move, but he's getting eaten alive. Soon Billy's screaming, "My bloody God, my bloody God. Get bloody off me."

> You see, for our purposes, the toughest man in wrestling is not the guy who can punch the hardest or match you move for move — it's the guy who would do anything to win a fight. Because in reality, he who bites first, bites last.

Baron Von Raschke: Guys like Mad Dog Vachon, they were tough guys.

Ronnie Garvin: Mad Dog Vachon . . . he'd bite the nose right off your face.

> All right we have two votes for the Mad Dog, but he was tough before most of you reading this book were likely even born. Let's continue.

Alan Funk: The Steiners. Scott Norton's also got to be up there.

Sid Vicious: People respect that guy, too. Steve Williams was always a tough guy until he got beat up by Bart Gunn. There's a guy, Bart Gunn.

Jimmy Valiant: You know some of the toughest when I broke in were Dick "the Bruiser" and then, of course, Verne Gagne. Then in the seventies, Bruno Sammartino. I wrestled all these guys. Pedro Morales. And in the eighties, of course, Jerry Lawler and Ivan Koloff. I mean, this is a tough business.

> Okay, we can see the Steiners being considered tough, but were you as shocked as we were that Jerry Lawler made someone's list?

We'll be the first to tell you that he's one of the nicest guys we've ever come across, but the toughest? Who knew? Actually, you'd be surprised at a lot of the names people mentioned, and what we came to realize is that each of them was tough in their own right. However, there was one name that came up time and time again. And surprisingly, the word nice also came up again.

Sid Vicious: I only know nice things about the guy. I've never seen him in a squabble, I've never seen him in a verbal argument, I've never seen him have any type of rage or anything in all the years I've ever known the guy. He definitely has the respect of everyone in the business.

PHANTOM

I have to interrupt Sid here for a second. Respect is a key word, something that should be kept in mind for this entire discussion. Perry Saturn is someone who has always been thought of as a tough guy, and in 1996 he came on our radio show as an in-studio guest. This was the first time anyone came into the studio, so Sir Adam and I were really excited. We got some muffins and coffee and thought everything would turn out great.

SIR ADAM

I still think we pissed him off by getting him muffins and not an energy bar or raw meat or something. He just doesn't strike me as a guy who can appreciate a good blueberry muffin.

PHANTOM

As he walked into the studio, wearing his ECW jacket, I knew something was wrong. He never looked us in the eye, never shook our hands, just sat down and started gulping down his coffee. As we went on air, he was responding to questions with yes/no answers and, mistakenly, I tried to liven things up a bit when we got wrestling legend Bob Backlund on the phone. Backlund started endorsing a more conservative view of the world; like that paddling should be reintroduced in schools. I disagreed and made some jokes at the expense of Mr. Backlund. All the while, I noticed Saturn shaking his head, looking down at the ground, obviously not getting the fact that this was part of the act. Backlund, on the other hand, got it, and we were going back and forth.

SIR ADAM

I sensed that everyone was in on the joke but Perry. It was radio shtick that must have gone over his head. He was fuming. Of course, I did nothing to stop it and let Phantom dig his own grave.

PHANTOM

At the end of the call Backlund said to me, "Maybe you wouldn't have such a smart mouth if I came down to the studio." With that, Perry Saturn added, "If you talked to me like that, I'd shove that microphone down your throat." I smiled at Saturn, happy that he was getting into it, but there was no smile back. Just the cold, hard look of death. And for the rest of the show I was convinced that Saturn was going to beat me within an inch of my life. Thank God nothing happened, and after the show Saturn just got up, shook my hand and left. I learned a valuable lesson, and it's not what you think it is: never joke around with a professional wrestler if they are standing in front of you. You never know who will get the joke and who won't. And that's respect. And what did this tough guy really prove, that he could make an out of shape radio host piss his pants?

SIR ADAM

Can we get back to the story? I want to know who Sid was talking about when you started another one of your therapy sessions.

Ted DiBiase: He's a teddy bear. He was one of the nicest guys you'll ever meet.

Scott Hudson: Easily one of the nicest guys. Just a dreamboat. Could not be nicer. Never saw him lose his temper.

Teddy Bear? Dreamboat? We know what you're thinking, are these guys kidding? How could those words describe a tough guy? And not just a tough guy, but a guy that strikes fear in the hearts of other tough guys.

Are you going to tell Meng his sleeveless shirt looks cheesy?

Kevin Sullivan: One time I asked him to do something which was completely wrong and he got a little upset. And, I mean, that was the scaredest I've ever been in my life. And he wasn't really upset. And I said, "Oh boy, thank God."

> Kevin Sullivan, the guy who used to pray to Abuddahdin, the guy who would stomp on people's stomachs for a finishing maneuver, was scared of a guy who's known as a "coffee buddy"?

Diamond Dallas Page: He would always [say], "Miss Kimberly, coffee?" He was her coffee buddy and she loves him and so do I . . .

> He made his pro debut in 1977, weighs in at around 295 pounds, and uses the Tongan Death grip as his finishing maneuver. The winner of the "I don't want to run into you in a dark alley contest," hands down, is Meng! Meng, Haku, King Tonga, one half of the Islanders, whatever you want to call him, he definitely has the respect of everyone we spoke to. Including the man he defeated for the wwf's King of the Ring title, Harley Race. It's important that Harley be mentioned, because his name came up almost as much as Meng's, and even over the phone you get the feeling that Harley knows about three hundred different ways of putting the hurt on you.

Harley Race: We finger wrestled one another. And to this day I've never been beat at doing that.

PHANTOM

> Oh that's cute, Harley and Meng, the two toughest guys, playing thumb wrestling . . . maybe I could join in?

SIR ADAM

> He can't possibly be talking about the innocent kind of thumb wrestling we did as kids.

Harley Race: Take your right hand and hook your left hand, just put your fingers together and start bending back and forth.

PHANTOM

Oh forget that, I was just kidding about it being "cute."

The strangest thing about our investigation is that everyone we interviewed for this chapter started out with only the nicest things to say about Meng. We almost thought we were being put on. It seemed like these guys were afraid to say anything really bad about him. However, people began to loosen up a little and, as more was said, things started to turn. Soon, we realized that this was the baddest motherfucker on the planet. Not Mike Tyson, not Jet Li. Meng is the toughest man in wrestling, and he could . . .

Bobby Heenan: Kill you more ways than my wife's meatloaf.

This is from his former manager, someone who traveled with him and went to bars with him. Oh no, we said bars didn't we? The one constant in the legend of Meng was that his fights usually started at a bar. And then things got really interesting.

Sean Waltman: He fought a bar full of people and twelve cops. Had to be maced before they could put cuffs on him.

Ted DiBiase: There was an incident in a bar in East St. Louis, which is a real rough part of town . . . One of the guys got into it and there were a lot of people involved and the police came. The big man had had a few drinks that night. And he's just trying to help and in the process of trying to help he gets maced and handcuffed. Now they handcuffed him behind his back and he broke the handcuffs. He snapped them.

Reno: If he's drunk, I would stay way the hell away from him. I've seen him and Goldberg go at it. They were both hammered when we were in England, and him and Goldberg went at it for fun. They were both hammered and they were just in the middle of the lobby rolling around. Then you got Ric Flair jumping on them, taking his pants off and running around.

PHANTOM

Why can't Ric just keep his clothes on?

SIR ADAM

I have no idea. So many promising stories end like that.

Hacksaw Jim Duggan: Meng has paid the price for having trouble out in the bars, because you never win a fight in a bar. At the very least you lose money. So I've seen Meng go, but I hate to give any special stories, because I know about the statute of limitations.

PHANTOM

Look at this. Hacksaw Jim Duggan is breaking out the legal mumbo jumbo. Come on, just one story! Everyone's done it, gone out to a bar, had a few too many, started talking shit, and sooner or later, you end up fighting with another drunken guy. Both of you throw some weak punches, and well, inevitably, you're sharing a whiskey sour with the guy, laughing about the whole situation. But not Meng, for some reason stories about him turn out a bit . . . differently.

Harley Race: There's six police officers in Montreal . . . Meng bit one guy's nose off; chewed on it a little bit. I'm not really sure what happened to the other guys. I know there's one guy who had an ear halfway tore off.

We'll bet Scott and Rick Steiner never learned how to suck in mace at college

Bobby Heenan: Took his two fingers on his right hand, his index finger and his trigger finger, and he reached into the guy's mouth and broke off his bottom teeth.

Jimmy Hart: In Hawaii one time, these policemen had come to break up a fight and he beat both of them up. Before it was over it took two or three police cars to come out and surround him.

Rick Steiner: I was in LA one time with him and he fought eight cops, they shot him with mace and he closed his eyes and sucked it in. He just opened his mouth and took in a deep breath. I mean, some of the stuff he did was like "What the hell?"

Bill Apter: I saw him put a fist through a wall in a restaurant where some fans were bothering him.

Alan Funk: I've seen the guy get smashed in the face with a chair about fifty times and the guy never even had a lump on his head. How the hell are you gonna hurt a guy like that?

Baron Von Raschke: You go into a bar and get in a fight? I don't think that makes you tough.

> Okay, Baron, sure that doesn't make him tough. If you're like the Baron, and still not convinced that Meng is Danger with a capital D, read some more of his credentials . . .

Matt Borne: Here's a 280–90 pound guy that's lightning fast with his feet. It's a pretty scary thought.

Bob Orton Jr.: He trained in all kinds of self-defense . . . and he's six-one and about a strong as a bull. That's probably a fella you wouldn't want pissed off at you.

Ted DiBiase: He is from the island of Tonga. He was sent to the United States from Japan.

What was he doing in Japan, you may be asking? Oh nothing much, just fighting as a sumo wrestler! The man is a three dimensional tough guy — and there are plenty of other legendary stories about him that take place outside of the barroom. Notice that many of these show he isn't just a fighting machine, but that he has a heart and respect for his fellow wrestlers.

Chris Candido: He was talking to me, Tammy Sytch and Chris Jericho. Up came Eric Bischoff and Greg Gagne and they walk right in front of us and start talking to Meng. He just looks at them and goes, "Hey!" And the entire locker room just froze. And I was like, man, these just weren't funny stories, apparently, he really is that tough. And he says, "Apologize to my friends, I'm talking." Everybody shut up and let him talk.

Jacques Rougeau: I was working against him. It was me and Raymond . . . Raymond gets in the ring, he has a spot with Tonga and . . . for one reason or another Raymond tags me in, but he tags me in too early. So I looked at Tonga . . . it must have been that time of the month . . . I locked up with him and by the time I had the chance to figure out what was going on he already had spinned me around and suplexed me on my neck. He's already on top of me like in amateur wrestling. I let him do everything he wanted to. I'm giving you my body . . . you do what you want with it.

Kevin Sullivan: One night I was booking . . . so I had to go tell these guys that they were going to do a job . . . They said to me . . . "What the fuck! This is not the right thing." Now they got themselves worked up, and they're saying, "Well, I don't know if we should do this. This is bullshit, holy bullshit, blah, blah, blah." Now it's starting to get a little worse. They said, "We'll kick anybody's ass here, blah, blah, blah." They keep going, "Why do you disrespect us? We'll kill anybody here." So I said, "Wait a minute, I'll go get Meng, he'll handle this for me." They said, "No, no, no, whatever you want, we'll do whatever you want."

Jake Roberts: I've seen him pull Jesse Barr's eye out.

Wait, what did he just say? That's a little intense, even for this chapter.

We knew this picture of Jesse Barr would come in handy one day

Kevin Sullivan: In Puerto Rico . . . this guy was working digging a ditch and they were walking down the street and Jesse went down the street with Meng and he kicked dirt on the guy. Meng said, "Brother, you shouldn't have done that." [Jesse] said, "Fuck you, what are you gonna do about it?" Big mistake. About three seconds later Jesse didn't have an eye.

Jake Roberts: It was really cool. But Haku is such a good man, he put it back in for him.

Taking a man's eye out? Does anyone need more proof of Meng's toughness? Of course, there is always a reason for the mayhem; Jessie Barr was making fun of a ditch digger, so he lost an eye. However, along with his toughest guy in wrestling reputation, Meng earned a rep for having a big heart, and that is also what earned the respect of his peers. And where is the man now? What can he possibly be doing?

Chris Candido: Ricky Santana is now semi-retired and selling cars with Meng, who got him the job. In their commercial, Meng is talking and nobody knows what he's saying. He's got a great big afro.

PHANTOM

Hey, after hearing these stories about the guy, I'd buy a car from him. I don't think I'd have a choice.

Dave Meltzer: I find it hard to believe that he'd be tougher than a Don Frye or a Ken Shamrock or a Mark Coleman.

Alright, Meng, that was D-A-V-E M-E-L-T-Z-E-R who said that — if you want to discuss it with him like two mature adults . . .
So, what does Meng have to say for himself?

SIR ADAM

For a while we considered finishing this chapter without even trying to interview Meng.

PHANTOM

We were both scared to call. Not just scared, petrified. I mean, how do you ask someone how he can break through handcuffs, suck in mace and pull out another man's eye?

SIR ADAM

But we found the courage and told him that everyone thought he was the toughest wrestler around. And he was pleasantly surprised.

Meng: I thank you for that and I appreciate it.

PHANTOM

It wouldn't do this chapter justice to have it just end here. As much as we wanted it to. We knew we had two more questions to ask. The first, why was it always Meng?

Meng: The fans, they challenged me when they had a few beers. We walk into a bar or walk into a restaurant, we kind of take the attention from the women. I take the attention from the local people. We can walk in, ten wrestlers into a bar, and they'll pick on me. It was always me — and Arn Anderson will tell you that.

SIR ADAM

It's just like Jim Duggan told us, Meng really didn't have much of a choice when he was out at the bars, people wanted to prove themselves and for some strange reason he was the measuring stick. They should have tested someone else. We'll buy that, but what about Jesse Barr? Did that even happen?

Meng: It happened. But it's sad because I always considered the boys as my family. They are my family. [When] things like that happen, to me, it's very sad. We should control it, but we're still human beings too.

As if you didn't have the chills already, we leave you with — what else? — a dark and twisted observation from Jake "the Snake" Roberts, who reminds us that we're all lucky to be sitting on a nice comfy couch reading this book, and not face to face with an angry Meng.

Jake Roberts: If I had a gun, and I was sitting in a tank, and I had one shell left, and Haku was three hundred yards away? He's mine, right? Well, the first thing I'm going to do is jump out of the tank and shoot myself — because I don't want to wound that son of a bitch and piss him off.

Chapter 3

Did the Kliq Control Wrestling?

Sean Waltman: Even though work conditions were miserable at the time — money was the shits, attendance was the shits — we still came into work laughing, with a smile on our face, five people in a fucking mini-van.

For this chapter we knew that we had to dust off our old characters, Detective Sir Adam Sipowitz and Detective Phantom Rinaldi.

DET. SIR ADAM

Who the hell is Rinaldi?

DET. PHANTOM RINALDI

Can't you ever just go along with it? To get to the bottom of this case, we interviewed wrestlers who were there at the time, guys like Chris Candido, Sid Vicious and Matt Borne.

DET. SIR ADAM

Then we got people who worked behind the scenes like Kevin Kelly, Jake Roberts and George Steele into the GIR interrogation room. And that's a dirty, dirty place.

DET. PHANTOM RINALDI

And then we got the Captain to get us a warrant to go backstage at Madison Square Garden to reenact the curtain call incident. That was my favorite part of this case, I'm so happy I got to be Nash.

DET. SIR ADAM

I can't believe I had to play George Steele while our engineer Ed got to be Shawn Michaels.

Just hearing the word clique can be enough to induce nausea in most people. Personally, for us it brings bring back memories of a catty group of high school girls who wouldn't give two aspiring wrestling radio talk show hosts the time of day. Certainly each and every one of us has had our own unpleasant run-ins with cliques during our lives. Which is why the word clique is not one that is usually followed up with kind words of praise. We would go as far as to say that not many independent-thinking people over the age of eighteen aim to be in anything that could even be potentially viewed as a clique, and we're not exactly going out on a limb by saying that the word is generally reserved to character-ize a group of people exhibiting shallow and infantile behavior. But other than that they're great.

Blackjack Brown: Just remember this. In wrestling, just like in any environment — it could be a cookie factory, it could be Avon — there's always a little clique . . . You want to be in that clique of guys that's getting pushed.

Sid Vicious: Yes there were cliques, they were obvious and they were silly.

Jake Roberts: There were several different cliques, there wasn't just one. There was two or three of them. You had the Samoan thing going on, you had the HBK bullshit, you had another thing going on. It was stupid.

Ah, the HBK bullshit. We were getting there, Jake.

SIR ADAM

Subtlety has never been one of Jake's greatest assets.

Damn, these guys must have had fun

Anyway, in the modern era of wrestling, there has never been a more storied group of friends than the five men who comprised what is known as "the Kliq." This unique group was made up of Shawn "the Heartbreak Kid" Michaels, Kevin "Diesel" Nash, Scott "Razor Ramon" Hall, Sean "1-2-3 Kid" Waltman and Paul "Triple H" Levesque. And just like with the Jewish Festival of Lights, there is more than one spelling for this group's unofficial name, and we will adopt the shortened version, with a K, because, well, it looks cooler. As wrestling rumors go, these guys were allegedly impossible to deal with, self-serving, drunk with power — and quite often just plain drunk. However, much of wrestling folklore is just that, a bunch of made-up stories. For years, we've heard and read that the Kliq ran roughshod over the then-wwf, helping each other at the expense of their fellow wrestlers within the company. And what we found is that the "truth" depends on who you talk to and how sensitive you are.

Justin Credible: In a way they did, they certainly controlled the WWF. They were an over, powerful group of guys, who were in top spots and stayed together. Yeah, they had that firm grip on it. I don't know if they controlled it, nobody controls it except the actual promoters.

Although Justin acknowledges that the Kliq was powerful and influential in its day, truth be told, he thinks that the stories regarding the Kliq's backstage politicking have been greatly exaggerated.

Justin Credible: I think it was a scapegoat in a lot of ways. The business wasn't what it was and there was a lot of blame going back and forth that the Kliq caused a lot of what was wrong with wrestling. And, you know, a lot of people were saying they were also what was right about wrestling, so you couldn't get a good in-between. It certainly was overblown, because those guys were more my friends than my enemies and I never got a push. So, if they were all powerful and could fire and hire people, I should have certainly had a higher spot, and I didn't.

Mystery solved? Well, we would be able to move on, but Justin was admittedly a friend of the Kliq, and was viewed by many as almost an unofficial member. So first things first, we had to know from Justin whether he was an unofficial member of the Kliq?

Justin Credible: Yeah, pretty much. I admired those guys, especially Shawn Michaels and Scott Hall. Their talents. I grew up a Shawn Michaels fan, even though he was in the AWA when I was growing up. So stuff like that is, you know, I just wanted to hang out with people who I felt were the best in the business. Just hanging around them you get to learn by listening.

In the interest of completeness we decided to press on and question a few more people and found markedly different reactions. Contrast Justin's comments with that of former wwf announcer and behind the scenes man Kevin Kelly.

Kevin Kelly: It controlled the WWF. Paralyzed the company. Not only did it have power in the wrestling end, but it had power in the office end. It was very difficult to get things done with those guys. They were such a fixture in the marketing plan and catalogs and magazines, if you needed stuff from them you had to set an appointment. They made you jump through hoops.

Now we're onto something. So did they control the wwf in the mid '90s?

Sid Vicious: Yeah, you know what? I think people like the Kliq always controlled it. But I was always friends with Kevin and those guys, but didn't consider myself in that clique. I hung around with a lot of different people, Undertaker wasn't in that clique. There were a lot of people who still got their respect. At the time, and I like all those guys, don't get me wrong, but they had their heads so far up Vince's ass it was impossible to see their ears. They called him every night. They called the dirt sheet writers and told them all the scoops and that's why they were getting all the praise. I was watching them read the sheets and tell me what they said to them.

Jake Roberts: My question was: "Vince, since when did you let the inmates run the asylum?" You got to have somebody in charge. There was nobody in charge.

Jeff Jarrett: It was a group of guys that had a deep-down passion for the business and at the time there was a lot of complaining and bitching and moaning going on. Payoffs were terrible, but that group of guys, I was friends with all of them, when the Kliq was at their so-called height, went out there and were trying to build a foundation.

> Surprisingly enough, what we found was that most of the complaints about the Kliq were not related to power struggles or devious plots to hold back certain wrestlers they didn't get along with. Instead, we discovered that many of the people who took issue with them did so because of their personalities.

Chris Candido: There's stories about them doing stuff with me and Tammy. But that's just guys being on the road for forty days. You're going to fuck with each other. It was very sophomoric stuff. They got to be the seniors in high school when I was the freshman and, you know, you just like to fuck with each other. And when somebody ribs you and you sell it, they rib you harder.

Matt Borne: They were suck-asses. Those guys, they would stab anybody in the back.

Wade Keller: I would say there was more resentment towards them because of the way they carried themselves. It didn't help when your leaders were so cliquish. I mean, there's a reason it was called the Kliq. They didn't name themselves the Kliq, other wrestlers did, because they would exclude others. It was very high school-ish, so they were resented.

> George Steele quit wrestling for the wwf in 1989, but went to work for the company as a road agent soon thereafter. In wrestling, the road agents are the guys responsible for overseeing the house shows all over the country. George had this to say about his dealings with the Kliq while a member of management:

"I hate the Kliq!"

George Steele: They would complain. If I forgot something when I was wrestling, then I forgot it. It was my responsibility to have whatever I was going to use that night there. So, like one night, Shawn Michaels, who's a great guy now, but boy he was a pain way back then for me — I just didn't really like him and he didn't really like me.

He was doing a thing where he was looking in the mirror to see who the most beautiful one was or some crazy thing. He had a mirror. And we had a truck that brought most of our things. But the truck didn't have a mirror in it. So he came running up to me. "Go get me a mirror." I said, "What the hell, there's a mirror on the wall." I knew what he wanted. He says to me, "They got to have one in the ring." I said, "Then go get it. You're the one that needs it, I don't." So he goes to Vince and says, "George didn't have a mirror there for me."

Jake Roberts: I had a few words with them, but usually they just turned and went the other way to the big guy.

Jeff Jarrett: They were guys who voiced their opinion and weren't afraid to do that. They didn't hide behind the "He said, she said" kind of things. They stepped right up front, and went into Vince's office.

> Ask any wrestler and he or she will tell you that the politics of wrestling is more than they bargained for when they first got into the business. With so few spots available and so many wrestlers vying for those positions, quite often it is who you know and who you've pissed off that determines your fate. It is because of this that most wrestlers believe that the talent should be separate from those booking the federation. Which is one of the main complaints we've heard about the Kliq, that they were too actively involved in the booking of many WWF storylines.

Jerry Lynn: I think whoever's booking shouldn't be wrestling at the same time. It'll just cloud their judgment or impair their judgment, because obviously they're gonna put themselves over so they're worth more money. If they're more valuable to the company they're worth more money. And always, whoever's their friend is going to get pushed. It happens no matter who's booking.

> While we're talking about booking, everyone in wrestling is looking for a shot to climb the ladder. A killer angle, a chance at the title, it can all be summed up in two words: a push. That's what drives wrestlers, being given an opportunity to shine and make the big money. And those who feel that they didn't get one, or that theirs ended prematurely are looking for answers and the name of the Kliq has been brought up on several occasions.

Jake Roberts: There were lots of guys up there that should have had a bigger push and lots of guys who shouldn't have gotten their push . . . As far as guys that I think should have [gotten] the push, the Headbangers should have had it.

The Kliq did everything from faking knee injuries when they didn't want to drop a belt to somebody, to simply refusing to give a belt up. Guess what guys? You are lucky to have it in the first place. I love this game, man, and I wrote television because I wanted it to be better. Not for a friend, not for an enemy, did I ever go the other way. I did stuff for people I couldn't stand, because my job was to help this business.

Jake Roberts and Sam Houston — fanny pack in tow

Ahmed Johnson (From an April 2002 *GIR Radio* Interview)**:** When I first got to the WWF I used to do a lot of high-flying stuff. Jumping off the ring and over the ropes, stuff like that. And I stopped because Shawn Michaels came to me one day and he was like, "Ahmed, you need to stop doing all this high-flying stuff." I'm like, "Why?" He's like, "'Cause when little guys like me get in there behind you it makes us look bad, so you got to stop that high-flying stuff." So I stopped. At the time Shawn Michaels was the king of the roost . . . But when he told me, I was taking it as this veteran guy helping me. And actually he wasn't helping me. He should never have told me that.

Chris Candido: I'm sure that guys they didn't like, they tried to screw over. Like Shawn himself in Germany, when the finish got screwed up, he told me, "When we get home the belts are coming off you guys." And when we came home sure enough the belts came off us.

Over the years, the most outspoken wrestler against the Kliq has been the former "Franchise" of ECW, Shane Douglas. Shane has come on the radio show and told us that he felt that the Kliq held him back when he arrived in the federation in 1995 as "Dean" Douglas, wrestling's very own professor. What the story boils down to is that Shane was supposed to get the Intercontinental title from Shawn Michaels. Michaels, however, was too "injured" to wrestle that night. As a result, Douglas was simply awarded the title — but subsequently lost it to Shawn's pal Scott Hall that same night. The Dean character never took off and many pointed fingers at the Kliq.

Shane Douglas: They wanted to keep the power in their clique. You know, if I come in there, let's face it, I've been a proven commodity in ECW, I've been a proven commodity in WCW, if I come in there and get the Intercontinental title handed to me, and I have a great run with it, guess what? It takes some of the power away from their clique . . . Because, without the weight of the titles, their clique isn't as effective.

Chris Candido: You know I can't say for sure, [but] part of the reason the Dean Douglas character apparently didn't get over was because Razor didn't want to work with him. He wanted to work with Hunter. So Scott wasn't giving everything he had in his matches with Shane.

Wade Keller: I think we've seen since why Shane Douglas wasn't pushed. It's 'cause Paul Heyman worked magic, making him seem better than he was. Shane's a good interview and a decent wrestler, but he wasn't a franchise. And he walked in there and obviously he didn't hit it off with the Kliq, but even if the Kliq had embraced him, I still think Vince McMahon would have looked at him and said, "You know, he's undersized, he's kind of awkward in the ring . . ." He's just not Vince's kind of wrestler. He just didn't have the style. I think that had as much to do with it as the battle with the Kliq.

DET. SIR ADAM

Personally, I always thought Shane was a great performer both in and out of ECW. He was a very believable heel. Even though I had spoken to him both on and off the air, when I saw him on TV I wanted to rip his throat out. If you can make me suspend my disbelief thirty minutes after talking to you on the phone about how ridiculous the cable bill is each month, you're doing something right.

Regardless of what side you take on Shane's WWE run, it's clear that when the Kliq was on top, they had power — a good relationship with Vince McMahon — and made things difficult for some people around them. But, has the level to which this stuff has been written about been blown out of proportion? You had a bunch of young guys making a considerable amount of money, living hard, acting somewhat immaturely and exerting influence that was handed to them by management. Did they really run roughshod?

George Steele: Oh, not really. They [just] weren't real respectful all the time — they would run to Vince like little babies. We were kind of in the middle, because they were very talented and, at the time, you got to remember most of us agents were [from] the old school, kayfabe type days. The business was changing and they didn't necessarily respect our beliefs.

Matt Borne: Okay, here's the scoop. When I was there, it was a clique, but all it really was, was three of four prima donnas riding the road together, wanting to solve all the problems of wrestling. I used to ride with those guys sometimes, and they would be putting each other over and telling each other how great they were. And there was Scott Hall talking about how everything should be booked, and what they're doing wrong, and the way they should be doing it. And I can remember sitting in the back seat rolling my eyes, going, "Holy Christ." Shawn Michaels was in the front seat, and every five seconds he's pulling down the visor, combing his hair. And I'm thinking, Jesus, you guys are believing your shit . . .

When Kevin Nash first came in — I can remember one of his first weeks with WWF — I was riding with him, Scott Hall and Shawn Michaels. We're in Jersey somewhere and we rented a car. We had about a three or four hour ride, we were going someplace up there in the Northeast. Nash is driving. He goes and gets gas. He comes out of the station and there's a median there, a curbed median. He wants to go the other way, but he can't go the other way, he's got to turn around someplace. He pops the median, bottoms out the middle of his Cadillac, and boom, he's fucked the car up. And I'm thinking, you stupid . . . If I would have been driving they would have been all over me! "Ah, Jesus Christ, what'd you do?" I'm sitting there and I didn't say a thing. They're just like, it's all right. Not even a mile down the road the car stops. It's messed up. Now we're in a bad neighborhood. We're in the hood. So we pull into this run-down complex, it looks like it was an old motel that was converted into apartments, and there's this pay phone sitting at what looks like was a check-in lobby. There's all these kids running around. Scott Hall gets out to make a phone call to call and get another car. So there are all these kids — it started out as about dozen of them — and pretty soon one says, "Hey, there's Razor Ramon! There's Razor Ramon!" So I'm just thinking Jesus Christ, hurry up, hurry up. So what do these guys do? They get out of the car. These other two guys get out of the car! "Hey, they know who we are!" They're out there signing autographs for all these kids in the hood and I'm sitting in the back of the car, just thinking, Jesus, you guys, you just don't get it.

That story makes them sound like nice guys who cared about their fans or, less altruistically, enjoyed their fame. Either way, they were the cool crowd and often screwed with those they didn't like, for whatever reason. We're not advocating this, especially in the workplace, but unprofessional behavior can only go on as long as management allows it. Which leads to the question: Why did Vince McMahon give them so much leeway?

Shane Douglas: From a booker's standpoint, the more shit that's going on in the dressing room, the more you're worried about fucking someone over on the other side of the dressing room, the less you're worried about your paycheck, the less you're worried about your spot, the less you're worried about all the important things. When something like the Kliq is raring its ugly head, and the guys are all pissed off, then nobody's going to Vince and saying, "My paycheck sucks." Vince is not a dumb guy, I think he used a lot of it to his benefit.

Sid Vicious: I'm sure Vince realized the business was down at that point. And this is the way they really look at it, too. When they've got that kind of time invested in a guy, even someone [Vince] disliked, he'd use him real well for a long time until he used him up. 'Cause that's the way he looks at the business. I think he enjoyed that Kliq thing because people were noticing it from the Internet. That was in the very first beginning stages of the Internet. And of course, it was all over the rumor mill.

Part of the blame also appears to lie on the shoulders of the other wrestlers themselves. The Kliq were only five guys out of an entire locker room, and there were other guys in the main events at the time who certainly wielded power.

Chris Candido: They were in charge because a lot of us let them be in charge. It's 'cause the business right around that time, from '94 to the end of '96, was kind of crappy. Everybody was always on edge: about what your payout was going to be; what towns you were going to be on. Those guys were hanging together [and] happened to be on top at that time. I mean, you always have power when you're on top, but also because a lot of the other guys were already in bad moods and leery about stuff so we'd put the heat on them in order to blame them.

Kevin Kelly: Mainly the biggest factor was that there was no one there at the time to step in and say, "Enough is enough, you've got to stop."

Occasionally, though, someone would stand up to the Kliq.

Matt Borne: Scott Hall was really bad. And I can remember when Shawn Michaels got suspended. He had dirty urine, for steroids or something, and Scott Hall had told Curt Hennig that I'm the one that snitched them off on it. How the hell do I know he's doing steroids? I don't give a damn. I wouldn't say anything anyway. So there was a lot of shit going on about that because Shawn got suspended for a little bit and Scott Hall whispered to guys in the dressing room: "Fucking Doink sucks. Doink's the one that snitched." Well, Curt came and told me about it, you know, and I ended up calling Scott on it . . . Well, his asshole puckered up, is what happened. I was mad. I was really mad. I was going through some personal problems myself. And then this kind of crap on top of it? I didn't need this kind of animosity.

Scott Hall? He don't have a gut in the world. I mean, if he thought he was right he would have stood up for himself.

Unfortunately, Curt Hennig has since passed away, but his legacy lives on. Not just his in-ring reputation, but also in his penchant for playing locker room pranks. The man is legendary in both respects and we'll never know if this story involving Borne was another one of his set-ups. After hearing about how Hennig likely started something between the Rougeaus and the Bulldogs that culminated in Jacques Rougeau knocking out the Dynamite Kid's teeth with a foreign object, we're not so sure. Nonetheless, it appears that part of the problem with the perception of the Kliq was that their attitudes weren't in line with those traditionally held in wrestling. With the advent of the Internet, they realized more and more that wrestling fans were in on the show. So, either they recognized the business was changing, or they changed the business.

Which bring us to what is referred to as the "Curtain Call." On May 19, 1996, at Madison Square Garden, Scott Hall and

Kevin Nash were working their last WWF show before leaving for WCW. Triple H had defeated Hall earlier in the evening and, in the main event, Michaels' defeated his bitter rival Nash inside a steel cage. It was business as usual except, following the main event, Shawn and his "enemy" Nash embraced in what was, at the time, thought to be an amazing show of sportsmanship. However, when Triple H and Razor Ramon ran into the ring and all four men then embraced and celebrated together, the audience was stunned. If you've never seen the video of this incident, picture the end of a Broadway show where the cast comes out and takes a bow to a round of applause. Except in this case, many weren't applauding.

Kevin Kelly: I remember Taker and British Bulldog being exceptionally offended by that, and both having to be restrained from going out to the ring while this was going on. Several guys took it very, very seriously.

George Steele: What was really happening was the whole system was passing us by. Four guys in the ring after a match, coming back and kissing each other wouldn't cut it when I wrestled. But it got over big time for them. Wrestling was changing, and to adjust, when we've done kayfabe most of our life and worked our business the way we did, well, it was really tough. Vince didn't have any idea it was going to happen. They had to come back the next day and apologize to all of us.

Not only weren't other wrestlers happy, but the Curtain Call incident clearly did not go over well with management either.

Kevin Kelly: It was very poorly received. I think Shawn's mind was so polluted at the time, that he didn't know right from wrong.

In 1996, the talk was that this incident would be the catalyst for the downfall of wrestling. But it was actually a glimpse into the future, setting the stage for the "reality" based comments and angles that carried WCW and WWE through the glory years of the

Did I ever tell you guys about the time I drove over a median in New Jersey?

late nineties. In fact, these days, if you stick around after a Raw taping, you're likely to see everyone in the locker room come out to wish Booker T a happy birthday. But the Curtain Call was ahead of its time, so someone had to be punished.

George Steele: Here's the situation: Shawn Michaels is the champion. What are you going to do to him? Razor Ramon and Diesel, they've already given their notice, they're going to WCW. So they only one that caught hell for a year and a half was Triple H. He wasn't the champion and he was the weakest of the four at that time. He was worried about his job. The other three were covered.

The next day I go to TV and [Triple H] calls me aside — I was very close to Triple H — "Jesus, Jim, am I in trouble?" I said, "Why?" He said, "I'm catching all the heat." I said, "Well, dummy, you did it. The other two guys are leaving and there's Shawn. Who's left to pick on?" He goes, "You know, you're right. Will I lose my job?" I said, "No, I don't think so, but you never know." I think he was scared . . . Well, he's married to Steph now. He's all right.

DET. PHANTOM RINALDI

George the Animal Steele was the only guy we could get who was in WWF management during this time? Shows you how much they appreciate what we do.

Although, for all intents and purposes, the Kliq dissolved once Hall, Nash and Waltman went to wcw, Hall's and Nash's power did not wane once they left the wwf. Still, it seems that, at least, this time their actions were better received by their peers.

Larry Zbyszko: Well it was easy for me, because even though you call them the Kliq, I'm the Living Legend. Guys like, well, Shawn Michaels, he got one of his big breaks, him and the other kid up in the AWA with the Midnight Rockers, and I was the champion up there and one of the guys that helped school them and worked with them sometimes and help develop them. Scott Hall, the same. He came in with the AWA. So they respected me. I thought they were great pals and they respected me for being the older guy who was an influence when they started. Which is the way it should be.

In fact, I noticed some big changes, especially in Scott, when he first came in from [WWE]. They were very grateful. They got a nice big contract, big money, more than they were making up in New York. And then everything got over really great.

Buff Bagwell: Things were so good at WCW. Everybody got along. There were no egos, no cliques. There was no: "Here we are, we're the money guys." Nobody gave a shit because we were all making money and the train was rolling. So nobody really cared. A lot of the stuff they created and made with the NWO angle was their idea. You gotta think of all the signals and signs Nash would do, like the

Wolfpack symbol, I mean that was all stuff he came up with. He made it cool.

Scott Hudson: Professionally? Run-ins? Negative? No, never. Never had a problem with those guys. The times I did meet them it was complimentary, or if I'm doing something with them, if I'm interviewing them on a Nitro or a Pay-per-view, it was just, "I want to get this over; what can we say to get this over?"

> This was a new Kliq. In fact, this Kliq even embraced the young up and coming talent and took them under their wing.

Reno: Kevin Nash was probably the coolest person I've ever met, or at least one of them. Kevin has such a camaraderie with the boys, he's one of the last old school guys. I can't say enough about him because he helped us. Literally, he took us under his wing, to the point where they actually put that into the show. All these guys, the older superstars and stuff, they were off doing their own thing. And here was Kevin, like our uncle or something, helping with all the young newcomers. And we were the ones who would stay up and party with him until five in the morning. We'd be sitting in his room and we'd all be huddled around him like school kids, him telling stories. He's one of the funniest people I ever met. I swear to God if he ever gets out of wrestling, he needs to go into stand up comedy.

> But this chapter would be incomplete without going to the source itself. Or in this case, themselves. We set out to find the Kliq and get their take. We tried all the local malls, but all we found was a new set of catty high school girls who wouldn't talk to us. And while we found numerous cliques, the closest we came to finding the "Kliq" was an old HBK poster and an NWO figure of Scott Hall in the bargain bin at the toy store. So we did what we had to do, we called WWE and asked to set up an interview.

DET. PHANTOM RINALDI

We asked to interview Triple H and Shawn Michaels for our book.

WWE said they would get back to us. We're still waiting for that call. Captain refused to get us a subpoena.

DET. SIR ADAM

I knew it was weird when Cap spit water at us when he denied our request. Realizing this was a dead end, we moved on.

Certainly two fun-loving guys like Kevin Nash and Scott Hall would talk to our lovable detectives. Right? And lucky for us, we were able to get Kevin Nash's cell phone number . . .

DET. SIR ADAM

It looked good. We had a lead on Nash and we thought we could make him talk. We were wrong. Kevin was less than happy to hear from us. While I rambled on about our case, and the "incident," all he wanted to know was where we got his number from. We were able to get around it by shifting the conversation to his acting career and how he was going to a premiere of a Josh Hartnett movie. Anyway, we got a laugh out of him and things looked good. He said we should call him back in a week and he'd do the interview. So we waited a week and tried and tried but always got voicemail.

DET. PHANTOM RINALDI

Foiled again. These Kliq guys are a sneaky bunch. I don't know what the hell we did wrong, but one week later the number was disconnected.

DET. SIR ADAM

I know what you did wrong. You refuse to acknowledge that cell phones show the phone number that's calling. You never leave a messages and people think you're a stalker.

So at this point we weighed our options. We started thinking about re-titling the chapter: "Did the Jive-Tones Control Wrestling in the mid '80s?"

Pez Whatley: What we tried to be was a Temptations entertainment angle. If you had a chance to watch our routine, what we done with the hat, cross the legs over, go down to the one knee . . .

The late Pez Whatley in full Jive-Tones regalia

DET. SIR ADAM

No, this wasn't going to work. We had to find a guy who had been on the show several times in the past. A guy who was always open, honest and candid. Sean Waltman.

DET. PHANTOM RINALDI

In what is probably the first bit of luck we've ever had, we called Chyna, and Sean was right by her side and happy to answer all of our questions. We fooled him. He didn't realize he was talking to the top pro wrestling detectives walking the beat.

(Excerpts from our interview with Sean Waltman:)

Sir Adam: Who gave you the name?

Sean Waltman: The Kliq? It was like, the other boys came up with the name because we were cliquish or whatever. The first time we ever heard the term clique used was J.J. Dillon coming to us and saying "You know, you guys can't be late all the time like you've been, because the boys are saying the Kliq is getting preferential treatment." That's the first time we heard that expression. Fuck, we hung out with a lot of people.

Phantom: There are a lot of rumors about the Kliq controlling wrestling in the mid '90s. Is this an overblown statement?

Sean Waltman: Without a doubt. The Kliq, apparently, did have some power. But I didn't. I wish I would've known, because I was the lowest paid guy on the fucking roster! You know what our power was? That nobody could break us. The only way they could break us was when guys left the company, but while we were there . . . We were just friends that drove together and talked about wrestling twenty-four hours a day.

Phantom: So do you think people were jealous that you guys were so tight and other people weren't as tight . . . because you were stronger in numbers?

Sean Waltman: Yes. They may not have liked us, but if they didn't like us, guess what? Okay, Shawn Michaels, he was a major asshole at times, but guess what, he was my friend; we accepted each other for who we were. Scott, when he got fucked up was very, very hard to be around. When I got fucked up I was just stupid. You know, everybody had something to say about us, but when they got in the ring with us, guess what, they had a smile on their face when they came back. We knew how to rock the house.

Sir Adam: People say the Kliq held back a lot of people . . .

Sean Waltman: Bullshit. If you're talented, guess what? Nobody can hold you back. Well that's not necessarily entirely true, but there were never any conspiracies to hold anybody back. That's bullshit. I

remember Shane Douglas blaming his failure in WWE on the Kliq, and I've seen Shane since and I get along with him fine. He's a good guy. But dude, sometimes you've got to look in the mirror and realize that not all your problems are because of other people.

Phantom: *Did you guys have booking power then?*

Sean Waltman: *A little bit.*

Phantom: *Could anyone have walked into these meeting or was it just certain people?*

Sean Waltman: *There weren't production meetings back when we were the Kliq, not like there are now. And when I was going to production meetings there, once a couple of us were going, at one point they welcomed anybody that cared enough to want to come in. But then it was pissing and moaning about information leaking or* *whatever. But really, I knew who the leak was, it was Paul Heyman. Dave Scherer on 1wrestling.com, I e-mailed him one time and I said: "Are Dave Scherer and Paul Heyman the same person? Because the shit that you're writing is verbatim the same fucking spew that comes out of his mouth."*

Sir Adam: *Why do you think he'd leak stuff?*

Sean Waltman: *He had his own agenda. I mean, this guy would go on e-mail campaigns and e-mail shit as other people with untraceable free Yahoo accounts.*

Phantom: *Who would he e-mail it to?*

Sean Waltman: *To the other websites.*

Phantom: *A lot of people say, back in the day, the Kliq was leaking stuff to the* Torch, *the* Observer. *Was that true?*

Sean Waltman: *No, I used to talk to Wade Keller, but I never leaked shit. If he would ask me about something that he heard and it was bullshit I would tell him it was bullshit. But I never compromised any information.*

Phantom: *Would he call you an unnamed source?*

Sean Waltman: *Sure, but I promise you, I'd never do what you're talking about.*

So in the end, many people blame Vince McMahon for allowing the Kliq to have too much power; others blame the wwf system. Us? The clues led us to one man, the guy who got everything started . . .

Rick Steiner: I actually got Kevin hired in the WWF. Vince asked me about someone for Shawn Michaels' bodyguard, and asked me about Kevin. I had his number and everything, and I said I didn't think he was under contract or anything. We ended up calling Kevin and he came out. That's when he came up as Diesel.

DET. PHANTOM RINALDI & DET. SIR ADAM

CASE CLOSED! LET'S BRING STEINER DOWNTOWN!

Chapter 4

Is Wrestling Genetic?

Kevin Von Erich: It was a family business.

Is Von Erich talking about *La Cosa Nostra*? Or was *The Partridge Family* his favorite TV show? No, he's talking about professional wrestling, and for as long as wrestling has been around there have been numerous real families involved. Father and sons, brothers, even sisters have gotten in on the act. Some successful (see Randy Savage), some not so successful (see Lanny Poffo). This got us thinking. Could there be a professional wrestling gene? No, not Gene Anderson, but an actual chromosome found in the DNA of the members of the Hart family or Funks that predisposes them to lacing up the boots and cutting promos.

PHANTOM

I may have failed Biology twice, but I'll be damned if I don't get to the bottom of this. Screw you, Mrs. McKenna. I always told you there must be a wrestling gene and I got a book deal to prove it!

SIR ADAM

Will you please stop? Don't take the title of this chapter so literally. And take off that lab coat. That thing hasn't fit you since the tenth grade.

PHANTOM

Where's my Bunsen burner?

Wrestling families are such an ingrained part of the business that many wrestlers actually pretend to be related just to get a rub off a famous last name. Ole and Arn Anderson aren't related to Gene; hell, they aren't even related to each other. And Ivan Koloff is no more Nikita's uncle than he is Russian. Unfortunately, many wrestlers get so accustomed to claiming that these essential strangers are their blood relatives that they don't even remember how they're supposed to be related. Yet they keep trying to hold on to what's left of the mystery. Take this bizarre conversation Phantom had with Jimmy Valiant of the world famous Valiant Brothers.

Phantom: Johnny Valiant and yourself, brothers?

Jimmy Valiant: No, we're not brothers.

Phantom: Friends?

Jimmy Valiant: Sisters. There's no difference between Johnny Valiant and myself. The only difference is, you know, I'm not luscious, I'm just handsome. And Johnny, he's not handsome, he's just luscious.

Phantom: Legitimately, you guys are brothers, right?

Jimmy Valiant: No. I'm writing a book and all this comes out in it.

SIR ADAM

What's scary is that Phantom actually had to ask if they were brothers in the first place. Should I break the news to him that D-Von and Bubba Ray Dudley aren't really related?

The Valiant sisters???

We all know the legendary families in wrestling. The Funks, the Ortons, the Von Erichs and the Mulkeys are just some of the multi-generational grapplers who became household names. But we were surprised at just how many wrestlers have a father, brother or grandfather in the business that weren't headliners, or even on the mid-card.

Chris Candido: Me and my grandfather, the not-very-legendary Popeye Chuck Richards of WWWF kinda Pete Sanchez/Johnny Rodz-level fame, were the blacksheeps. My family never wanted me to get into [wrestling] because of the way it made my grandfather, who I happened to love. He was, you know, an idiot. And I wanted to be that. And I think I finally reached that level of idiocy.

All right, so Chris Candido's grandfather never reached the heights of a Dory Funk, Sr. or Larry Hennig, but that wasn't enough to stop Chris from wanting to follow in his footsteps. Surely, Popeye must have had some flashy road stories to make such an impression on young Chris.

Chris Candido: My grandfather and Little Louie, broke into, you know, them cabins where you go fishing through the floor and the ice. There was a whole area of them at this place where they were working and somebody was just never using theirs. So instead of living in an apartment, my grandfather and the midget Little Louie broke into someone's ice fishing place and they lived there for, like, six months. In a way, I was almost drawn to the anti-glamour. My grandfather lived in an ice hut, and when he was retired he sold microwaves in JC Penney's. And he was a great big man, who would die his hair blonde until the day he died and walk around saying, "You like this microwave?"

Seeing your grandfather living in an ice hut and hardly making a living is something that would turn most people off. But it actually encouraged Candido. Whether it was because his grandfather was larger than life, or just the sheer lunacy of it all, doesn't matter — we believe Candido never really had a choice. There must be something about pro-wrestling that gets passed down from generation to generation, not in a learned way, but inherently, just by being around it.

Matt Borne: We seem to understand the intangible things. Sometimes we just understand because we grew up around it. Like Dustin Rhodes — I just clicked with Dustin [and] Curt Hennig. All the guys that are second generation, and that have been around since they were kids, we just see things a little differently than guys that just break in. Even guys that break in and are destined to become stars, they don't see it, they don't understand it. It's something that's deeply imbedded in you at a young age. I can't really put my finger on any particular attribute, it's just some intangible.

PHANTOM

See, even Matt Borne says it's DNA.

SIR ADAM

You're going to take genetics lessons from Doink the Clown?

Sounds like Matt is talking about something he was almost *Borne* into . . . And like Candido, Matt didn't have a WWE Hall of Famer to watch while he was growing up. His father was "Tough" Tony Borne, just another wrestler collecting a paycheck to feed his family.

Matt Borne: My dad never sat down and explained the wrestling business to me, I was taught a little bit at a time. I can remember really clearly the first time that I really started understanding it. I was five, six years old, and John Tolos was in the dressing room. I walked in behind my dad, and John scooped me up, gave me a backbreaker . . . and then slammed me onto the bench . . . I felt this punch to my head and it didn't hurt me . . . all I was was dizzy. And

I thought, damn, I just got the shit kicked out of me and I didn't even feel it! Here I was, a kid, understanding the business — and I was watching these fans that were grown adults believing every damn thing that they saw.

PHANTOM

When I was growing up, my brother and I would watch wrestling, then practice what we saw on each other. We'd wrestle for hours at a time, ending up with bloody lips and busted eyes. We'd buy the magazines, rent the Coliseum Videos and watch the Pay-per-views. My brother is now a financial analyst and I am a fringe wrestling radio show host who never wrestled a match. But we were die-hard wrestling fans, so why didn't either of us become wrestlers? Is it because our father is a pharmacist, and his father a dress salesman?

It is exactly this contradiction, between Matt Borne's and Phantom's family lives, that explains why Matt was the one who donned the lumberjack outfit and became Big Josh in wcw. Matt saw wrestling as a potential career because he was exposed to it on a daily basis. For Phantom, it was more of a fantasy world.

Jimmy Garvin: I think sons see their fathers come home in the limos, living the high life. Money grows on trees if your dad is a top worker. Kids see that. "Why should I go to school for five or six years? I'm going to take my father's name, take a few bumps and get some strings pulled. I'm going to have an easy career too."

PHANTOM

I got it. Wrestling osmosis. The professional wrestling gene is so powerful, much like Gene Anderson, that just by spending time around a wrestler, it's passed on through witnessing the magic first-hand. This theory is going to make us rich.

Jimmy Garvin and Squeezie

SIR ADAM

I'm starting to agree with you. Geneticists all over the world will soon be recognizing our work. Where's my lab coat?

PHANTOM

Under the newly formed GIR theory of wrestling relativity, it need not even be an actual blood relative to influence a future grappler. We set out to test our new theory on the Garvin family. Jimmy used to see his stepfather Ronnie, wrestling on the top of the cards, and that must have lead him to lace up the boots and start his own professional wrestling career.

Jimmy Garvin: Didn't influence me whatsoever. Ronnie and I went our separate ways, I left home when I was 14, so I raised myself. I went to Canada. met my wife up there when I was 16, turned pro in Arizona with no help from Ronnie. Our paths came together because promoters worked it out that way. We get along, but we don't go out to dinner together.

SIR ADAM

There goes your theory. I knew you were full of crap.

So while *GIR Radio*'s favorite "brother" tag team of all time weren't even brothers, the thing that surprised us more was that they really didn't even like each other. Was the wrestling business to blame? This was something we had to find out for ourselves so we tracked down the elusive Ronnie Garvin. Here's what he had to say about his stepson Jimmy:

Ronnie Garvin: *He was a 14 year old kid and I was 22 at the time, and I was doing my own shit and he was doing his.*

Sir Adam: *So the mother must have been older than you?*

Ronnie Garvin: *Oh yeah.*

Phantom: *How much older?*

Ronnie Garvin: *Oh lord, she was an old douchebag. She was, I can't remember, 14 years older.*

Phantom: *You're a stud!*

Ronnie Garvin: *Yeah, I guess.*

SIR ADAM

I can't blame Jimmy for not buddying up to Ronnie if those are Ronnie's terms of endearment for Momma Garvin.

PHANTOM

Even though Jimmy says that Ronnie never influenced him, it still remains that Jimmy didn't become a doctor or lawyer.

Jimmy Garvin: I'm a captain on the sixth largest airline in the world — don't want to say which one.

Ronnie Garvin: I went into flying. I've been flying for like 35 years.

You mean you could fly Delta to Florida and have "Gorgeous" Jimmy Garvin as your captain, and fly TWA back and put your life in the "Hands of Stone" of Ronnie Garvin?

Ronnie Garvin: It's cargo. A freight business. And I'm self-employed there.

So while Jimmy says that Ronnie wasn't an influence, it's very hard for us to believe. Not only did Jimmy take up the same profession as his step-dad, but even in retirement they're both doing basically the same thing. In Jimmy's case, it's not really genetics at work, but rather his environment — just like it was for Ted DiBiase.

Ted DiBiase: I grew up in and around the business. Mike DiBiase was actually my stepfather. He married my mother when I was like four, but he became the father figure in my life and he was a good one. And not only was he a good professional wrestler, he was a national amateur champion. And so that played very big in my mind and heart. I loved the man dearly and I just wanted to emulate him as much as possible.

It is undeniable that professional wrestling is a very political business. Having a well-established family member within the sport, not only to influence you, but also to pave the way, definitely helps.

Rick Steiner: We both wrestled in college, in high school . . . I had some influence, I guess he kind of watched and saw what I did and the type of money and things that were involved. And it gave Scott an avenue, easier access than him having to do it all by himself.

Bob Orton: He (Bob Orton Sr.) tried to discourage me a little bit, but that didn't matter. That's what I wanted to do so I did it. But he did open up the door.

Eddie Guerrero (From an 11/01 *GIR Radio* Interview)**:** I grew up in this business. It's a part of me. And it's something that I still have and I don't want to lose it 'cause I love it.

Jake Roberts: My father wrestled in this business for a long time. I have a half brother and a half sister. When I went to New York, Vince called me and said, "I'm thinking about bringing your father in, and your half-brother." I said, "Vince don't hire them for me, because it ain't about that. Do your job, I'll do mine. Your job is not to give my family jobs."

Second generation grappler Bob Orton, Jr.

SIR ADAM

Leave it to Jake the Snake to contradict any theory we come up with.

Just like life, wrestling and wrestlers can't always be explained by neat little theories. Everyone is different — especially Jake. He had other family-related reasons for getting involved in the sport.

Jake Roberts: I didn't want to be a wrestler, I wanted to be an architect, but I thought, you go out there and become a wrestler and maybe he'll (Grizzly Smith, Jake's father) like you.

As with all things Jake, this is part of a darker side of getting into wrestling after your father. Upon entering the sport, Roberts met with a unique set of challenges — they almost seem like a wrestling angle. These issues were not just emotional, but also physical.

Jake Roberts: When I started wrestling I got my ass kicked because a lot of guys couldn't kick my dad's ass, so they took it out on me. My dad was 7 foot, 450. Okay, I'm 6–5, 240. They had an axe to grind with him and I got some of it.

After taking beatings meant for his dad and becoming a more successful wrestler in his own right, one would think that Jake must've earned Grizzly Smith's respect. However, their relationship is far from perfect.

Jake Roberts: I don't talk to him, I don't see him. I love him, but that's the way it is, man. I was wrong expecting a certain type of love, I was expecting *Leave It To Beaver*-type love.

It would be unfair to say that Jake's is the only dark story out there. There are plenty we stumbled upon, completely by accident. In 1996 a young third generation WWF superstar who went by the name of Rocky Maivia was on *Get in the Ring Radio*. Of course, fans all over the world now know him as the Rock.

PHANTOM

He came on to promote an upcoming WWF show at the Nassau Coliseum, and just to demonstrate how much of a non-entity he was in his rookie year, Sir Adam and myself weren't even that excited to have him.

SIR ADAM

Earlier in the week, we told the WWF that we would rather have Marc Mero on the show. As usual, they ignored our wishes. So we put on a happy face and welcomed Rocky with open arms.

The Rock: As far as teaming up with him (Rocky Johnson), we discussed it after WrestleMania. Right now I don't feel it's in my best interest to team up with my dad.

PHANTOM

> As ridiculous as this sounds now, at the time we were surprised at how good of a talker he was. Everything was going great until our engineer accidentally hung up on him mid-interview. We hung up on the Rock! But even back then the Rock was a class act. He actually called back and then went into detail about his dad and his plans for his career.

> And was he ever right. By not making a name off of his father, the Rock was able to create a whole new persona for himself. He never really had to deal with being pigeonholed as "Rocky Johnson's kid". We found what he said next so interesting it took us almost eight years to follow up on it. (We never claimed to be anything but lazy.)

The Rock: I was always by my father's side. Let me put it to you like this, my father was nothing like Dusty Rhodes.

> The Rock touched on what is an all-too-common aspect of having a parent in the wrestling business: the bigger the superstar, the more absent he/she is from their child's life. To be the offspring of a wrestler has its advantages at times, but it also comes with a tremendous amount of pressure.

Dustin Rhodes (From a 1/04 *GIR Radio* Interview): [Goldust] definitely was edgy and it had never been seen before. It was pretty "out there," but yeah, I gave it a try. I didn't have a problem with it. It was nice to get away from my dad's shadow, you know, to try to do something on my own, something that's never been done before. I did something on my own and I'm very proud of Goldust and what he did for me.

If you doubt the effect having a famous father can have on someone entering the sport, think about this: the only way Dustin Rhodes could get out from under the shadow of Dusty Rhodes was to portray a gold-painted, cross-dressing, bisexual. It seems natural that there would be some resentment or jealousy of Big Dust, and Dustin is begging for a chance to prove himself against his dad in the ring.

Dustin Rhodes (From a 1/04 *GIR Radio* Interview)**:** You know what I want, deep down in my heart, is to wrestle against him. My dad, you know, I talk to him about it all the time, and he's like, "I'll never do that. No, forget it, uh-uh." It's a pride issue with him, I guess, but I mean I would love to do that.

Dustin's not alone. How about being the son of Ric Flair? Carrying that last name into the ring is an unbelievable burden.

David Flair: What he's accomplished, people expect you to succeed at his level. It's kinda hard because no one has, and no one will. It's kind of just thrown at you. I'd only been in the business a couple months, and then just thrown on TV . . .

Unfortunately, we all had to witness David Flair's initial matches in wcw. While they were eager to put together big-name father vs. son matches, the powers that be either didn't realize or didn't care that David had no real in-ring experience. Still, while David appeared intimidated by the burden of the being Ric Flair's kid, many thrive on such a challenge.

Bob Orton Jr.: I never thought of it as a burden. I thought of it as an accomplishment, becoming as good as my dad.

Most of the wrestlers we've come in contact with have strong opinions as to whether or not they would want their children involved in the business. For instance, what would Bobby Heenan have done if his daughter wanted to become part the world that made him a very rich, very famous man?

Bobby Heenan: I think you would have found the words Smith & Wesson in the roof of her mouth. First of all, she would never have said that, 'cause I would never raise her that way. I have always explained to her that education is more important than anything I did.

> Wow, that's a strong statement, and not what we expected. How about some more from other guys who reaped the benefits of main event runs, who made a good living in wrestling.

Jimmy Garvin: I'd clothesline them . . . I don't want them to pay those dues. You start at the bottom and work your way up. I don't want my kids going through that.

Ted DiBiase: Over my dead body. I told them, if you can't respect me and accept my knowledge of the business and what I've learned from the business, if that is not enough, you will be on your own, you will get no support or help from me. If you want to go do it yourself, I'll be here when you come back. I will forever cherish my years in the business, and the wrestling business was extremely good to me. When I say that I don't want my children to follow me, it's just that I saw what it can do. No father wants that for his children or wants them to even take that risk. When you line up the success stories with the stories of misery and failure, the misery and failure stories far outweigh the ones that end happily.

Shane Douglas: I would clearly try to steer him away from it. I'd let him know exactly how crappy this business has been. Everyone wants their sons or daughters to aspire to be better than they were, and have more, and I honestly don't think the wrestling business is going to be able to dish out the kind of living that I want my son to have.

PHANTOM

No child of mine will ever, ever get involved with professional wrestling radio. It's driven me insane. It gets me so mad just thinking how long it actually took to get recognized enough to get this book deal. The worst part of it for me is that when a wrestler says he'll come on the show — eighty percent of the time, when it comes to getting them on the phone, they aren't home.

SIR ADAM

Every night I cry over my daughter's crib and pray silently that she is not sitting in some dingy radio studio trying to explain why the Iron Sheik, Jr. couldn't come on the show this week. Damn that Sheik. Damn him!

Of course, there are some guys out there who want their names to live on — at least a little while longer. If there weren't, then the age of second and third generation wrestlers would be over. But seriously, who would ever want to get involved in a business where those involved wouldn't want their own kids to do it?

Jacques Rougeau: Maybe some people are not proud of what they do . . . My great uncle, Eddie Auger, was the first. And then my uncle, Johnny Rougeau, who was very famous, then my dad, Jacques Rougeau. My brother Raymond Rougeau, my brother Armand Rougeau, wrestled with us. My two sons are wrestling now, J.J. Rougeau and Cedric Rougeau.

PHANTOM

There's so many of them . . . I think I may be a Rougeau.

SIR ADAM

Who the hell is Eddie Auger?

Bob Orton Jr.: I grew up around the sport and so did Randy and that, by and of itself, would probably make somebody lean toward it. Especially if they're as athletic as Randy. I'm all for it. That's what he wanted to do, and I was behind him all the way.

Sid Vicious: If they decided to do it I'd be behind it 100% . . . My youngest son, he says he might be a wrestler.

That's more like it. Wrestling can't be all bad. Pro wrestling isn't a bad place to earn your keep.

Sid Vicious: I would tell him: "This is what you can expect." And even if you're better than other people, it's not gonna matter. It's like you're on an assembly line: you do what you're told and . . . more often than not, you'll stay around.

PHANTOM

Ahhh, fatherly advice from Sid Vicious.

Of course, there's something that can be said about trying to force wrestling on your children. Today, the Von Erichs are a family synonymous with tragedy. Five sons passed away at an early age, and three committed suicide. Today, only one remains. Many wrestling journalists claim that Fritz Von Erich was like a drill sergeant, forcing each of his sons to become a professional wrestler — even when they really didn't want to — and that it lead, ultimately, to the family's downfall.

Ted DiBiase: I have a tendency to think that Fritz expected his boys to be in the business.

Kevin Von Erich and his late brother, David

Jeff Jarrell: I guess you can say his actions speak for themselves. It's such an unfortunate situation. Our families worked together when we went to Dallas — it's very tragic.

King Kong Bundy (From a 2/97 *GIR Radio* Interview)**:** It's horrible what their father did to them. He's a horrible man. He pushed those guys. The one little skinny one was particularly sad 'cause he had no aptitude for the business. He was about 160 pounds, and [Fritz] just pushed him into it anyway.

> Since Fritz has passed on, we talked to the only remaining Von Erich, to get his side of the story.

Kevin Von Erich: Being little boys, you know, we loved our dad, and we wanted to do what our dad did. But actually, I wanted to play football; Dave, basketball; and Kerry track. We didn't want to be part of something that we considered kind of hokey. We wanted to get in there and we wanted to hit as hard as we could and we wanted to get in the ring and do like we'd been doing in NCAA. Give 100%. And we just stayed off the nose, teeth and balls. The low stuff. 'Cause you had to wrestle this guy tomorrow night. And so everywhere else, any muscle mass, we would hit as hard as we could. And we'd really lay into them. We really didn't want to be into it, but we started wrestling as a kind of summer job — a summer job that lasted 19 years. Dad didn't make us wrestle, or beat us, or force us. He was really a good, honorable man — but he did see it as a business. And, lets face it, like any business, sometimes you don't want to do it.

Kevin sheds light on what many have alleged was an underlying tension in the Von Erich home — that the kids should follow in their father's footsteps because it was good for business. In fact, even after the death of a brother, the surviving Von Erichs had to perform in the company's memorial shows.

Kevin Von Erich: Once a brother would die, you'd have to get in the ring. And the last thing you'd want to do was beat the hell out of that guy across the ropes from you when all you're thinking about is your brother.

But what was behind the suicides?

Kevin Von Erich: Kerry was arrested (for cocaine possession). And that just tore him up inside. He hated that. And that's really the reason Mike committed suicide. He got caught with a joint and that was after he had already had that fever and he had stomped a parked car in and tore down a signal light. And he would do that for maybe a week and then he'd go four weeks and he'd be normal again, but that 106 degree fever had burned his brain and made his decision-making ability not what it should be. It was thinking that you had let your brothers down, your mother and father down.

While so many Von Erichs went into wrestling, the Jarrett family seems to have taken a different approach. Like Fritz Von Erich,

Jerry Jarrett controlled an entire territory, but Jerry never forced his kids into anything. In fact, out of three brothers, Jeff Jarrett was the only one who even decided to embark on a career in sports entertainment.

Jeff Jarrett: He let me make up my own mind. Really, in every conversation I remember, he was never, "Hey, do this." He'd be inquisitive about what I liked or didn't like. As far as pushing, no.

Jeff really has followed in his father's footsteps. He now runs TNA, completing the circle, from wrestler to promoter, just like his father before him.

Jeff Jarrett: I would definitely, without a doubt, say that genetics is the least likely characteristic that would make you a successful performer. I think it has more to do with passion and environment. If you're around it, whether you come from a wrestling family, or whether you're a die-hard wrestling fan, like Mick Foley, that grew up watching wrestling, you've really got to have that passion. There have been a number of miserable failures, guys who stepped into the business because their father or their uncle or someone preceded them, who had several things going for them. So I do not think it's a genetic thing, there have been more second generation failures than successes.

SIR ADAM

We've learned a lot in this chapter, but since our agent just informed us that our application for a federal genetic research grant was denied, we must cut off our work here.

PHANTOM

There are clearly many different ways of looking at this mystery. And after reading this chapter you probably have your own theory. One thing is for sure, Mrs. McKenna should have realized my potential.

SIR ADAM

Here goes nothing.

Mrs. McKenna: Unfortunately boys, after reading your paper, I am forced to give you yet another "F." Your hypothesis is patently ridiculous. Despite being twelve years older, nothing has changed as far as your lack of adherence to the scientific method I described in detail while the two of you drew up fictitious wrestling tournaments in the back of my class.

SIR ADAM

I told you she would never forget. Now we'll never get a better grade.

Mrs. McKenna: The fifth step of the scientific method is to draw a conclusion. Scientists draw conclusions by examining the data from an experiment. There are basically two possible outcomes, either your experiment supports the hypothesis and can be regarded as true, or the experiment disproves the hypothesis as false. If your hypothesis is false, you must repeat the steps in the scientific method and make adjustments to your hypothesis. And by the way, Barry Windham would never have beaten Ricky Steamboat in his prime.

Chapter 5

Why Does Steve Austin Hate Jeff Jarrett?

Joanie "Chyna" Laurer: Are you kidding me? That is some serious, stupid shit. Steve Austin wouldn't wrestle Jeff Jarrett because he didn't hit the ropes hard enough? Get a job! Get a job, Stone Cold!

In wrestling, there's nothing better than a good rivalry, a long, drawn out feud. A number of classics come to mind: Bruno Sammartino vs. Larry Zbyszko, Mick Foley vs. the Undertaker, the Hardy Boyz vs. Edge and Christian and, of course, Steve Austin vs. Jeff Jarrett. What? You don't remember that one? Well, neither do we. But that's one of the great things about having your own pro wrestling radio show, sometimes you uncover storylines that never even made it past the dressing room door.

In 1997, Steve Austin was the hottest wrestler the WWF had on its roster. Single handedly, he sold more merchandise, Pay-per-views and tickets than any other world champion before him. Steve had the wrestling world in the palm of his hand, and had earned the rare right to say "No." (Not only to writers, road agents, and assorted office workers in Titan Towers — Austin could actually say "No" to the boss, Vince McMahon.) He was able to call his own shots, and because of that, wrestling fans all over the word were deprived of a Steve Austin vs. Jeff Jarrett feud.

Bruno Sammartino and his old nemesis Larry Zbyszko

At the same time, Steve Austin put the kibosh on any hopes of Jeff Jarrett ever getting to the main event level in the World Wrestling Federation. Several years later, questions remain. Why did Austin decide Jeff Jarrett was not worthy? Who wanted the feud to happen? And, more importantly, is the whole thing even true, or is it yet another wrestling rumor? First things first: it happened. When he was on *Get in the Ring* in late 2003, Austin went into detail as to why he felt Jarrett wasn't the right guy for him to wrestle.

Steve Austin (From an 11/03 *GIR Radio* Interview)**:** He wasn't physical enough — he didn't hit the ropes hard enough. And it wasn't a case of me being able to bring him up, more a case of him bringing me down, because of how hot I was. I'm not out there UFC shoot fighting, but Jesus Christ, lay some stuff in on me, bust my mouth, whatever. That's the way I did it when I was feeding comebacks on DX and all those guys. I mean, guys would be walking backstage with busted lips and noses, loose teeth. I was throwing sledge hammers in there and people were going crazy — that's just the way it was.

Ken Shamrock: [Jarrett] is definitely old school. He's definitely lighter than most. But then again, a lot of boys like that. He had a pretty boy act, but with everything that we ever did I was happy.

Larry Zbyszko: Saying that someone would bring you down or whatever is kind of an excuse — the boys would say that if they didn't want to wrestle somebody.

> This wrestling rumor or, for purposes of this book, "mystery," brings up an interesting question. Should a heavyweight champion be able to call his own shots? While no one can argue that Vince McMahon is and was the boss, the fact is, he wasn't able to convince Austin to work a program with Jeff Jarrett. McMahon couldn't fire Austin because, at the time, Austin's character was making the wwf millions of dollars. Like Hulk Hogan before him, Steve Austin was able to have complete control of who he took with him into the main event and, more importantly, who would share the lucrative Pay-per-view payoffs that came with those main event slots. You've already read about the Kliq and the amount of influence Shawn Michaels, Kevin Nash, Scott Hall, and Sean Waltman enjoyed in the mid-'90s. But in 1997, it was Steve Austin who put his foot down, and wwf fans were subjected to yet another Undertaker/Stone Cold feud because of it. The chairman of the board lost his ground and this allowed a superstar — one that he created — to call the shots. It makes you wonder about other intriguing match ups that may have been squashed by Steve Austin's veto power. On a smaller scale, ECW learned from the wwf's situation.

Tod Gordon: [ECW] never wanted to be in the position that Vince McMahon was in, where an Ultimate Warrior or someone like that could say, "Hey, I'm not going out there versus Jarrett, and I'm not doing the job unless you do XYZ for me right now. Forget it, I'm not wrestling tonight. I'm walking out." We never wanted a wrestler to be bigger than the promotion. Which is why they yelled "ECW, ECW" and not "Shane, Shane, Shane." They didn't go "Raven, Raven, Raven," they went "ECW, ECW, ECW." It was the product. We could put on a show and not announce one match and sell the same number of seats as if we had announced the entire card. No one star was ever going to be bigger than the product. No one was irreplaceable.

Maybe that was possible for a smaller scale promotion like ECW, but the WWF was concerned with the millions of dollars they had invested in marketing "Stone Cold" Steve Austin. In a tight spot, they almost had no choice but to appease him. Of course, the other side of the coin is that Steve Austin was paid a lot of money by WWE and part of his job was to wrestle who they wanted him to and, at times, to help create new stars. There was a time when the World champion would be expected to . . .

SIR ADAM

I know, I know! "A champion should be able to wrestle a broom and make it look good." How many times have we heard that said over the years? I still think the 1983 Ric Flair vs. Wooden Broom match in Charlotte, NC, was the worst match I ever saw in my life.

PHANTOM

I totally disagree. It was a mat classic. I actually believed that Wooden Broom would take the strap that night.

With this book, we should now be considered wrestling scholars. So as much as we like Austin, we couldn't take his rejection of the "Broom Theory" at face value. We had to consult other experts in the field, and find out what they thought of the theory. Right Professor Hoggarth?

SIR ADAM

You didn't take your medication while we wrote this thing, did you?

PHANTOM

Come on, let's just be Professors, I got one word for you —
COEDS!

SIR ADAM

So Professor Phantom and I decided to reach out to a good friend
of the show, Professor Lawrence Zbyszko.

Prof. Larry Zbyszko: When I was the champion, it didn't matter who
came in, I could work a match with guys like Greg Gagne who could
do a high spot and flip around or I could work a match with a guy
like Nikita Koloff who is more of the big, mean, tough guy. But to be
a good worker you had to mesh your style with how the other guys
could work. That was one of the secrets of being a good worker. A
good worker had to look at the opponent and say, "Ok, this guy can't
do this, so we'll work the whole match in another way."

PHANTOM

Then we had to consult with another, maybe even more respected
"broom theory" proponent . . .

SIR ADAM

Dr. Harley Race.

Dr. Harley Race: I took George Gulas, who looked like a human milk
bottle, and I made him look like a winner for sixty minutes. His
father walked back to the dressing room after it was over and shook
hands with me and there were some hundred dollar bills in it.

PHANTOM

Sir Adam, the man's a genius. With just one answer he came up with another possibility — the "Milk Bottle Theory."

Dr. Harley Race: I believed in myself, enough that I knew I could make a milk bottle look like it could wrestle. Maybe Steve didn't have that confidence.

Now we were on to something. After this last statement we were convinced that Harley Race, the poster boy for "the Broom Theory," was on Jeff Jarrett's side. He believed that Jeff Jarrett was worthy, a top guy who should have had the opportunity to work with Austin.

Dr. Harley Race: Jeff and his father both, neither one of them, should have really been in the wrestling business. They backed into it due to a relationship with the Welch family. Jeff became a decent worker. The only reason why he was ever, ever used on top was his father owned the promotion.

SIR ADAM

We were wrong there, but who can blame us? Harley Race is one of the hardest guys to get a read on in this business.

PHANTOM

Yeah, well, at least we know he's not a big fan of Steve or Jeff.

Dr. Harley Race: I told WCW that by letting [Austin] go when they let him go they were making the dumbest decision I ever thought they were gonna make. And he went on to prove me right. It was just something about him. The way he carried himself.

SIR ADAM

See what we mean?

There's two sides to every story — and sometimes three. In 1997, Jeff Jarrett was hitting the glass ceiling in the wwf. He was a mid-card wrestler who started getting true "crowd heat" — the fans really began to hate him. Certain members of the office recognized this and decided that it was time for Jeff Jarrett to become a big money player. Which is precisely when the political games began backstage, turning Jeff Jarrett and Steve Austin into chess pieces for the power brokers.

Kevin Kelly: Russo was always pushing Jeff very hard. So when Russo was writing TV, it was, "Let's get Jeff to do this and that." At the same time, Jim Ross was very strongly in Austin's corner. Ross and Russo were very strongly opposed and Russo was trying to take away a lot of Ross's power in terms of making matches. He took away Pay-per-views, started to look at who got talent pool payoffs, all the things that were controlled by JR.

SIR ADAM

Since, to our knowledge, this was the first main event match being played out in a book, we had to get the other participant to comment.

PHANTOM

According to Sir Adam, getting Jeff Jarrett to comment on this situation was one of the hardest things we had to do to in writing this book. I still don't see what the big deal was.

SIR ADAM

Jarrett's a promoter now and we can't just get him on the phone like we did in the old days. He's got a PR department, and I must have left a dozen voicemail and e-mail messages with them. For three months, every time I spoke with them, they said Jeff would do it — soon. We needed this interview badly, so I was more persistent than I've ever been before. And then, the one day in three months that Jeff was available, Phantom gets to do the fun part.

PHANTOM

Finally, it happened. Jeff was going to be available from 3 to 3:15pm — and Sir Adam had to dispose of someone.

SIR ADAM

That's *depose*, not *dispose*. You make it sound like I'm a hit man, not a lawyer.

PHANTOM

So it was up to me.

SIR ADAM

I told him not to start out with the Austin questions — just ease into it — maybe it was a sore subject with Jeff.

PHANTOM

So I started right away with the Austin questions, and luckily he didn't hang up. And unlike Sir Adam and me, it seemed Jeff really has gotten over the past.

Jeff Jarrett: It was very confusing, you sort of scratch your head and think: okay, I've got to hear a real legitimate reason why this guy doesn't want this to happen. Because to this day, I still haven't heard one that truly makes business sense.

PHANTOM

Nervously, I played Steve's comments to Jeff.

SIR ADAM

And for some reason you played them for DDP also.

PHANTOM

Yeah, I just wanted to hear DDP's reaction, the guy's funny as hell.

SIR ADAM

Jeff Jarrett showing his "Stone Cold" critics how to throw a punch

No matter how much you kiss his ass, he'll never introduce you to Kimberly.

PHANTOM

Damn!

Steve Austin (From an 11/03 *GIR Radio* Interview): He can't hit the ropes hard enough to bust an egg, I had a violent, physical work style. I mean Jesus, you want to work with me, bring it!

Diamond Dallas Page: Did [Steve] say that? Austin and Nash, those guys don't give a fuck. They'll say whatever the fuck they want, and I respect them for that.

Jeff Jarrett: Steve Austin has drawn a ton of money and throws a very phony punch. This business is all about perception. So I really don't understand that one, still, to this day. There's a lot of things that you can pinpoint, or complain about, in Jeff Jarrett. But his in-ring work? I've never heard that. This statement about hitting the ropes confuses me more than him not wanting to work with me.

> It confused us also. Having never wrestled, we didn't even know what Steve really meant. Luckily, we talked to some experts — men who have managed to crack an egg or two — on a rope — in their day.

Larry Zbyszko: Steve is one these guys that go full bore. And some guys who had that style used to look at other guys and go, "Oh, he doesn't hit the ropes hard enough."

Diamond Dallas Page: Steve, in his prime, that motherfucker was a rocket. I mean, holy shit, he would hit those ropes like a fucking cannon.

Sean Waltman: When you are going off the ropes you need to have good velocity. But Jarrett made up for it other ways.

Chris Kanyon: The more I think about it, I don't think Jeff hits the ropes all that hard. I don't know why you wouldn't want to wrestle someone because of that. Everybody has a different type of style. I don't know if Steve was using it as a metaphor, that Jeff doesn't work hard in there . . . Rob Van Dam doesn't run the ropes hard, if you watch him. Actually, Raven said it on commentary once, when he was doing *Heat*. Whoever was commentating with him said, "Rob's real fast." Raven pointed out, on air, that: "Actually, if you watch him, he doesn't move that fast in the ring. His arms and legs are fast when he does kicks and stuff, but when he runs the ropes he's not that fast."

Rob Van Dam (From a 10/03 *GIR Radio* Interview)**:** And that's the coolness that's R.V.D.

Now we're really confused, where did Rob Van Dam come from? Anyway, something just wasn't right. Could this really have been the only reason that Steve Austin didn't want to wrestle Jeff Jarrett? That Jarrett's style wasn't as explosive as Austin's?

Sean Waltman: There were personal reasons why Steve wouldn't work with Jeff — and it wasn't because he didn't hit the ropes hard enough.

SIR ADAM

You read our minds Sean. During our interview with Steve it became apparent that he just didn't like Jarrett. When he was talking about him, the tone in Austin's voice changed; like he was talking about someone he considered a piece of garbage.

PHANTOM

Austin had the same tone in his voice that I have whenever I talk about Sir Adam.

SIR ADAM

There had to be more, something that happened in their past.

Steve Austin (From an 11/03 *GIR Radio* Interview): I remember one time, in Evansville. There were little cubicles we'd hang out in, and at the time I had a hundred dollar a night guarantee — and that was a lot of money back then. One day I go in my little cubicle in Evansville and I'm looking at my check and it should have been, like, 600 bucks, because I think I worked six shots that week. And I think it was like 350 or 400. I was just looking at it, deadpan, in shock. I'd been starving forever down there and now I have a chance to buy me a damn turkey or something . . . Jarrett comes [over], looks at my check, slaps me on the back and says, "It ain't gonna grow by looking at it."

I was like, "You son of a gun."

Jeff is the son of Jerry Jarrett, who owned and operated the Memphis territory when Steve was starting to make a name for himself. Jeff, being the son of the owner, was put in a position of power that many resented. Certainly, Jeff's position didn't warrant taking such a cheap shot at one of the wrestlers in their stable, but, more importantly, did Jarrett even remember this incident?

All he wanted was a damn turkey

Jeff Jarrett: Not at all. I do know this, that Steve probably didn't like the payoffs that any promoter he's ever worked for have given him. He's probably complained to Vince McMahon about payoffs. I would think that he's got issues with every promoter [he's] ever worked for.

As it turns out, this wasn't the only incident involving Jarrett and Austin that never made its way on to television. In 1998, Vince McMahon signed Jarrett away from WCW, and in an effort to create a buzz, McMahon instructed Jarrett's first interview to be a shoot. Jarrett was to speak from the heart about why he left WCW and what he didn't like about the WWF performers. In a statement that, after reading this chapter, can't be thought of as a coincidence, Jarrett's first victim was "Stone Cold" Steve Austin. He began to talk about how he thought Austin's new catchphrase of Austin 3:16 was "blasphemous", and how the WWF should be ashamed of it. If you need any proof that this was a legitimate shoot, keep in mind that Austin was floored by the comments and wasn't afraid to let Jarrett know he was upset.

Kevin Kelly: I was there when Jeff Jarrett returned and came out and gave his famous little shoot promo thing in the ring where he said that he felt that Austin's 3:16 was blasphemous, which is what Jeff's opinion truly was. But [Jeff] was instructed by Vince Russo to speak his peace . . . When Jeff came through the curtain, Austin was pretty much right there, and he said, "You're talking about my merchandise, you're talking about my money and I don't like it." What Jeff probably should have done was gone to Steve and said, "Hey, listen, this is what they want me to do, and what do you think about it?"

SIR ADAM

After hearing stories about where the bad blood came from, we thought it only fair to find out more about Steve Austin, the man behind the "Stone Cold" character.

PHANTOM

We wanted to paint a complete picture of his personality.

SIR ADAM

Oh great, let me guess, break out the smocks, now we're going to be artists. How about psychiatrists?

PHANTOM

No, that was a metaphor. You're really losing it, aren't you?

Ronnie Garvin: I met him one time and I think he's a very nice guy. It was his first Russian chain match; I had hundreds of them. Austin said, "How do you fight, what do you do with a chain?" He was lost. I was impressed that he asked me that. It was kind of an honor.

Erik Watts: Austin came up to me — we were doing long matches for a while. One night, they were going to have him put me over in a town. And I remember him and Grizzly Smith going at it and Grizzly saying, "Hey man, you know his dad will fire you." And Steve goes, "Bill Watts can do whatever the hell he wants, I'm not gonna put him over. The kid's not at my level. He doesn't deserve to be put over." He did it a million times with me. I remember it was me and Dustin Rhodes that were gonna wrestle Austin and Pillman, and I was real young. And Austin said, "Have you got the finish yet?" And I go, "No." And he goes, "Well I haven't either, but I can guarantee you two things in this match. I can guarantee you, one, I'm gonna whip your ass, and I'll guarantee you a brush with success. Because you're gonna brush up against me and I'm success."

> During his tenure in wcw, Steve Austin was a confident performer, even if he wasn't always at the top of the card. Despite never really becoming a main event player, Austin knew he should have been. Shortly after getting fired from wcw, Austin emerged in ecw and created waves with his cutting edge promos. To get a better feeling of where his head was back then, before he became the international superstar he is today, we talked to the guy who started ecw, Tod Gordon. Tod had an interesting story of how Austin handled a situation that, when read now, falls in line with Austin's old school mentality.

Tod Gordon: What happened was, apparently, without my knowledge, Austin and Paul Heyman made an agreement. He did not want to get in the ring following a match where there was blood. A promise like that, unless he's on first every night, would be very hard to keep, because ECW was a bloody federation. There was always going to be blood. So he felt he was lied to. And the next show, he just plain no-showed. And for some reason Paul felt he couldn't call him and ask him why. So I did, and Steve told me, "The guy made a promise to me, he lied. So that was a receipt." So I said, "Don't you think you could have come up to me and ask for some make good?" That was just bad business.

> Austin subscribed to an old wrestling adage: when someone does something wrong to you, they must get a receipt for their actions. No misdeed goes unpunished. Now, it seems like Steve was waiting for the right time to get revenge for that fateful day in Evansville. That is, unless he forgot about the whole thing . . . .

Kevin Kelly: When Austin made it big, and he's got a memory like an elephant, he never forgot the guys that helped him get there or hurt him along the way. So when he has the opportunity to put the screws, financially, to Jeff Jarrett, by keeping him out of the main event program, he did just that.

PHANTOM

I guess we can safely assume that Steve didn't forget.

SIR ADAM

Just like you Phantom, you always hold a grudge. Even after all these years you still hate Perry Saturn.

PHANTOM

Please don't mention that guy's name, he's dead to me.

SIR ADAM

All right, it's over. You know, it's funny to think that one of the perks that came along with Austin making it as far as he did was that he could get back at people like Jeff Jarrett.

Ted DiBiase: I did foresee him becoming the big star. As a matter of fact, I told Steve. I can remember when I was managing him as the Ringmaster, there were a lot of the agents there telling him that he wasn't doing enough in the ring. That he needed to be doing more high spots and stuff. And I said, "Steve, do not change anything." I said, "What you're doing now is wrestling. This is going to sound crazy, but wrestling today is different. And it makes you different than everybody else. And you don't want to come from the cookie cutter. You don't want to be like everybody else." I said, "You have a rugged style, and it's an on the mat style, and it's realistic."

> If you believe everything you read, then it seems like everyone knew Steve Austin would become a main-eventer years before it happened. The Jarretts are included in the long list of Austin supporters — something which maybe even Steve doesn't know. Then again, maybe he doesn't care. More likely, to Austin, the Jarretts will always be the guys who made money when he had none.

Kevin Kelly: Steve Austin harbored a lot of bad feelings toward Jeff Jarrett because of the fact that Steve was starved when he was down in Memphis, while Jeff was catered to as the booker's son. Jerry had this huge mansion in Hendersonville, and both of them lived a good life, while Steve was getting around on forty bucks a night.

Jeff Jarrett: As far as him and my dad having a run in, I will not dispute that at all. But I do know this as a fact, that my father and Chris Adams handpicked Steve out of the wrestling school. My father handpicked him to come from the Dallas area, when we were running the Sportatorium, to come to Tennessee and learn. He can have his problems with me, but to have a problem with the guy who was very instrumental in his career says a lot about where the guy's head is at. And where his heart's at.

> While the situation played itself out behind the scenes, in front of the camera it was business as usual. As far as the WWF office was concerned, Steve Austin's next opponent was going to be Jeff

Jarrett and storylines were written as such. Austin, on the other hand, had different plans. He decided to make a stand in Cleveland, Ohio. Fans will remember it as the night Ben Stiller appeared on *Raw*.

Steve Austin (From an 11/03 *GIR Radio* Interview)**:** I was hotter than hell and then they bring this Ben Stiller guy out. "Okay, Steve, you're gonna go out there and save Ben Stiller." And I'm like, "No, why the hell am I gonna save Ben Stiller? What did the hell did he do for me?" I said, "Oh, I don't care, I'll save Ben Stiller." And they said, "Then you'll give Jeff Jarrett a stunner." Give Jeff a stunner? Ok, I'm already thinking this out — I'm gonna give someone a physicality, a stunner, so there's gonna be something down the line. Right? Because you just don't have me go out there and give a guy who's looking for some action a stunner and then just cruise along on your way.

Dave Meltzer: It was in Cleveland's Gund Arena. He got everyone in a room and said, "Look, I've been saying this, I'm not going to take myself down. Because it will take the specialness off of me."

Steve Austin (From an 11/03 *GIR Radio* Interview)**:** Then we get to the Gund Arena and they said, "Okay, Steve, we want you to work a match with Jeff Jarrett. I said, "What? You want me to work with who?" They said, "Jeff Jarrett." I said, I think Vince Russo was telling me this, I said, "Alright, come here." So we walked into McMahon's room, it might have been me, Vince, Jim Ross and about five other people. I said, "F this." M, S, F. Those were the best damn cussing jobs. I said, "I told you son of a bitches that I never wanted to work with the guy. And now you're gonna make me come here and play the bad guy."

SIR ADAM

We tried to get Ben Stiller to talk, but our calls to his agent went unreturned.

What did you expect, the guy makes a movie every week — he doesn't want to dredge up the past. Especially when it revolves around the time he made an appearance on *RAW* to promote *Mystery Men*. That movie sucked.

Jeff Jarrett: To me, it comes down to professionalism. You truly separate your personal feelings from your business feelings. Vince McMahon is the best ever at that; he can separate almost in an uncanny way. Steve is someone who, obviously, has never been able to do that.

> We've established that Steve Austin didn't like Jeff Jarrett, and that he made up his mind that Jarrett would never reach his level. The question still remained, did Jeff Jarrett deserve the main event slot? Or was he a wrestler who always should have competed at the mid-card level?

Dave Meltzer: It wouldn't have killed [Austin] to work with Jeff Jarrett — he was still gonna be Stone Cold. But at the same time, it wasn't in the best interests of anyone but Jeff Jarrett and Vince Russo for that program to happen. So to me, when it happened, it was like: Is this the right thing for business? And I thought at the time it was. Other people would disagree, but I just didn't think Jarrett was at that level and it was gonna hurt Austin to be working with him.

Erik Watts: Is Jeff a main-eventer? Absolutely . . . I love to watch him as a heel.

Ken Shamrock: In Jeff Jarrett's defense, obviously he's been around a long time, he deserved a shot.

Wade Keller: Jarrett was a step down for him, because he wasn't going to be in headline matches against Jarrett.

Sean Waltman: Jeff didn't hit the ropes the hardest, but I could tell you bad things about my own work. You can pick anybody apart. He's a great worker, I had great matches with him. I love him.

SIR ADAM

This is very hard for us at *GIR Radio*, because both of these guys have been great to us in the past and have been on the show on numerous occasions. If this chapter was Why Does Steve Austin Hate Ted DiBiase? there would be no problem. Anyway, my usual barometer is if a wrestler gives a great interview, he's championship material in my eyes.

PHANTOM

So that's why you're always talking about Sharkboy being the uncrowned World Champ?

It becomes obvious that Jeff Jarrett deserved a run — maybe a brief one, but a run at the title nonetheless. Austin wanted to get back at Jarrett and did a really a good job of just that. Not only wasn't Jeff Jarrett working with the world champion, but instead, he had to lose his Intercontinental title to a woman. Mind you, that woman was Chyna, and she could beat the crap out of both of us at the same time. However, when it happened to Jarrett she was an inexperienced wrestler. And, of course, there has always been a stigma attached to losing to a female in a competitive sport.

Joanie "Chyna" Laurer: Jeff Jarrett was very good with me. As a matter of fact, I enjoyed it. I wish I could do a kitchen match now. I would kick his ass, because I had just started having my own matches at that time. Really, I felt so much pressure and didn't have the experience I have now . . .

Jarrett became a sacrificial lamb when it became clear he intended to leave for WCW. Chyna became the first female Intercontinental champion after pinning him in a "Good Housekeeping" gimmick match. Recently, Jeff became the promoter for TNA wrestling. If you don't think Jarrett learned anything from his dealings with a world champion who had the ability to call his own shots, think again.

"I can't believe you guys squeezed a whole chapter out of this."

Jeff Jarrett: What we're trying to do in TNA is have many different opponents, many different styles, and the champion has to adapt . . . It's what made the great champions so good — Harley Race lasted for years because he could wrestle all styles. Brisco could, Dory and Terry could, Flair could. You know, these guys could wrestle many different styles, and that's what made them.

PHANTOM

And Steve Austin went on to become my close personal friend.

SIR ADAM

You're still sticking with that?

PHANTOM

Of course, when he left WWE I called him up and asked him to come on our show. Since then we've spoken many times, he calls me Phantom, I call him Steve.

SIR ADAM

And to this day he hasn't come back on the show. In fact, he's even gone back to WWE.

PHANTOM

He's just waiting for the right opportunity.

SIR ADAM

So when he comes on I can say he was crazy to hold onto his grudge for so long and not give Double J a shot?

PHANTOM

You're crazy, Austin earned the right to burn anyone he felt like burning, and the reason he's my bud is he probably remembers what I asked him when he was on the show the last time.

Phantom: Would you have rather worked with Ben Stiller than Jeff Jarrett?

Steve Austin: Well, Ben Stiller's got a hell of a drop kick. I don't know . . .

SIR ADAM

I can see it now, Austin versus Stiller in a steel cage.

PHANTOM

Now you're talking!

SIR ADAM

As far as this mystery goes, Sean Waltman sums it up best.

Sean Waltman: If you are one of the very few guys in the industry that can call his own shots and you're not hurting business for everybody else by doing that, then damnit, do it! And if you don't want to work with somebody because you don't like them personally, and you have the power? Fuck it, don't wrestle him. But don't say it's because he doesn't hit the ropes hard enough . . .

Chapter 6

Was ECW the Best Wrestling Promotion Ever?

Rob Van Dam (From a 10/03 *GIR Radio* Interview)**:** ECW is a time that's gone, unfortunately. I can only hang on to as much of it as I can . . .

EC Lon: ECW still exists, I am waiting patiently for the next *November to Remember*.

Sure, it's telling when a current WWE Superstar reminisces about his days working in a smaller promotion. But what's more amazing is that someone in his thirties, who actually re-named himself after that same small, now defunct, promotion, still logs on to www.ecwwrestling.com every day, only to stare at a blank screen. What do Rob Van Dam and a disturbed *Get in the Ring Radio* regular have in common?

They both cling, fondly, to memories of Extreme Championship Wrestling.

PHANTOM

Better known as EC Lon-a-hue, EC Lon pops up on our show

every few months. He lives, sleeps and breathes ECW. He had a psychotic breakdown when it went out of business.

SIR ADAM

He actually lost it on the date the company filed for bankruptcy, April 5th, 2001. To this day, he refuses to acknowledge that ECW has gone out of business. He still calls us and starts talking about fictional matches that are going to take place at Wrestlepalooza.

PHANTOM

He even takes credit for inventing "the chant." To hear someone this psychotic on the radio is actually very entertaining. It also illustrates a scary point; there are other ECW fans who were similarly affected by the promotion.

RVD, Tazz, Bill Alphonso, and Sabu during ECW's heyday

Johnny Grunge: Sick individual. They probably were a part of something and felt: ECW, that's mine. This ain't Hulk Hogan or Ric Flair, this is ECW . . . I'm a part of it.

> There are what seems to be thousands of wrestling fans who aren't ready to let go of the legend of Extreme Championship Wrestling. At least not yet. Turn on *RAW*, or even TNA, and wait until someone goes through a table or gets hit with a chair. Chances are you'll hear the chant: "EC DUB, EC DUB, EC DUB." Even as you're reading this book, you can be sure that somewhere, somehow, there's an ECW chant breaking out. What was it about the promotion that captured the hearts and minds of hardcore wrestling fans everywhere? Was it really that good, or have four years of inactivity been kind to its legacy? Was it the best promotion ever, or will it become yet another footnote in wrestling's history, much like Joe Pedicino's GWF, Herb Abrams' UWF, the AWF, or Smokey Mountain Wrestling? If you're looking for an answer, you really need to start at the beginning. ECW was first known as Eastern Championship Wrestling and was founded in 1992 by Tod Gordon.

Tod Gordon: We were the Howard Stern of wrestling—that was my concept at the time. Everybody else was doing cartoons. My concept was, why is Howard Stern now in Philadelphia and Washington? How did this guy get into nine markets? Nobody was in nine markets. The reason is, people were craving an "R" rated radio show. And it hit me, that's what's missing, an "R" rated wrestling show. That was my first creative instinct, long before Paul Heyman and I converged.

Shane Douglas: At a time when wrestling had become so ridiculous, so cartoonish, in 1992–93, suddenly, here comes a company that's telling you to cut the fucking music and girls fighting in the ring. Instead, it's chair shots and blood, tables being broken and Sabu flying like nobody's ever seen in the States before. Plus we told everyone, "Bring your pessimism with you instead of leaving it at the front door." We said, "Bring it on in," and all those fans that brought that pessimism with them walked out believers. What we gave them was realistic enough that you didn't have to sit there and go, "God, the guy missed by three feet, but he still dropped." Instead, we were laying stuff in tighter than had ever been done in the States before. And that's why the fans bought into it.

PHANTOM

I think the reason ECW became so successful so quickly was the Philadelphia fans. For some reason, the fans there are rabid. I still remember the time in

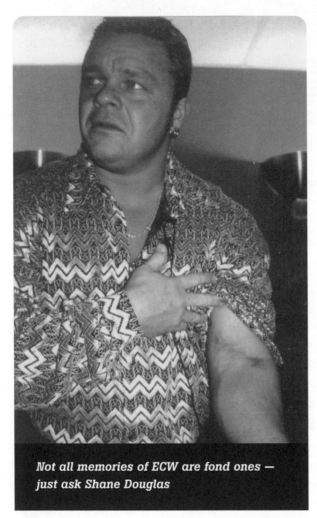

Not all memories of ECW are fond ones —
just ask Shane Douglas

1989 that I was visiting a friend in Philly who had tickets to Halloween Havoc. I wasn't hosting the radio show at that time, and had only been to WWF shows. I was shocked that the fans were cheering whoever they wanted to cheer — that the heels were getting huge reactions. Sid Vicious was cheered, while Lex Luger was practically booed out of the building. Muta was greeted like a returning hero while Sting had garbage thrown at him. And the roar of the crowd helped the matches, the wrestlers seemed inspired and it created an unbelievable feeling, being in the audience.

Terry Funk (From an 8/96 *GIR Radio* Interview): There are incredible fans up there. They really are. There aren't better wrestling fans anywhere in the country. And I'll tell you something else, they're connoisseurs of wrestling, too. You look at Rey Mysterio. Would he have had the opportunity that he's having now, or Guerrero, or any of them, if they didn't go up there and wrestle before the hardcore fans of ECW?

SIR ADAM

When I first saw video tapes of ECW, the chant is what really got me into it. It was infectious, it was almost like every match on the card was an event.

EC LON

EC Dub! EC Dub! EC Dub!

Today, the chant is still heard at WWE events around the country — and it's been four years since ECW folded.

Tod Gordon: Has it been only four years? Seems like it's even longer than that. I think they're still chanting because it's their way of stating that ECW was what revolutionized the sport of professional wrestling. And they want that feeling back — no other product has ever given it to them — a feeling that it was an interactive promotion, a promotion where the fans were literally a part of the show. That drove us to do certain things. I think they'll always chant, as long as there are people around from the company. Until the last guy out there is done, I'm dead serious. It could be Stevie Richards, it could be anybody.

Sean Waltman: They had the most loyal following. I mean, think about it, once ECW was gone, it was like the legend of ECW got huge, you know? All of a sudden people are chanting ECW in the WWE.

They had such a strong thing that they even incorporated it into the WWE, and WWE liked it enough to buy their video tape library.

EC LON

EC Dub! EC Dub! EC Dub! I can't wait for Living Dangerously 2005! EC Dub! EC Dub!

SIR ADAM

Why is he in our font?

AJ Styles: The name of the company was cool to say . . . I do not think ECW would have been as popular as it was if it weren't for the fans—the fans are what made ECW. If they hadn't run in Philly, who knows where they'd be right now.

Chris Kanyon: I don't think the chants mean anything. I'm a big New York Ranger fan and to this day in the Garden they chant "Potvin sucks." Does that mean that Potvin was the worst hockey player of all time? No. Just means that the chanting caught on.

Shortly after starting in Philadelphia, Tod Gordon's right hand man, the late Eddie Gilbert, left ECW. Gordon replaced him with a wrestling personality most fans knew as Paul E. Dangerously, a manager in WCW. But Paul Heyman was more than just a manager — he was a student of pro wrestling. And when he began booking for the federation, ECW started showing even more of an edge.

Tod Gordon: I brought him in, I guess late '93 early '94, up until the end of '95, which I consider the glory years of ECW. It was a total joint collaboration. After '95 I would say it was much more an 80/20 percent split.

After Heyman took over the creative reigns, he put some radical new ideas into play. In the finals of an NWA Title tournament that

The ECW world title belt

featured stars from many independent promotions around the country, Shane Douglas defeated Two Cold Scorpio for the belt. However, instead of gloating over becoming the champion of the prestigious and legendary organization, Douglas threw down the belt and proclaimed himself the first Extreme Championship Wrestling world champion. The story has always been that only Shane Douglas, Tod Gordon and Paul Heyman knew this was going to happen, and that NWA promoters were infuriated. Regardless of whether or not it was a true shoot, the fact remains that Shane Douglas's actions got fans talking about ECW. Then the wrestling became more violent than in any other American promotion. Sabu and Public Enemy became poster children for ECW's violence, utilizing tables in a way that most fans had never seen.

Johnny Grunge: I always tell everybody, we didn't start using tables, Sabu started it. We never took credit for starting it. Sabu, I'll tell anybody to this day, Sabu was the first one to do it — it was Sabu's gig. And at that time he left and went to Japan, and Paul came to us and said, "Guys, try it. There's no Sabu, we need to make the people happy. They're used to seeing it." To tell you the truth, the first time I did it I was scared as hell. I'm like, "Man, going through a table? Then going to the floor? What the hell?"

SIR ADAM

No matter how many times you've seen it, when someone gets put through a table, it's awe inspiring. You wonder how they're not dead — or at least broken in half.

PHANTOM

Since this is a book about solving mysteries, we wanted to get some quotes from Sabu, the innovator of table spots. Unfortunately, he refuses to talk to us. Actually, he refuses to talk to anyone in the wrestling media. He's one of the few workers left who holds onto his gimmick outside the ring. These days, even Abdullah the Butcher will speak — and even he talks about ECW.

Abdullah the Butcher (From a 5/02 *GIR Radio* Interview)**:** I started all the hardcore. I'm the one who used the garbage pails. Me and Bruiser Brody and the Funk Brothers. We're the ones who started all this.

SIR ADAM

Here's how our most recent attempt at interviewing Sabu went. It must have been our fifth call. The interesting thing is he answers his phone, so we know he can actually talk . . .

[The phone rings . . .]

Sabu: *Hel — (Note: He doesn't even complete the word.)*

Sir Adam: *Sabu, this is Sir Adam —*

Phantom: *And the Phantom, from* Get in the Ring *radio.*

Sir Adam: *We're really huge fans (Note: This is how we butter up a potential guest.)*

[Silence . . .]

Phantom: *Really big fans.*

[Sabu breathes . . .]

Sir Adam: *We're writing a book now, and would love to include you in it. Do you have ten minutes to do a quick interview?*

Phantom: *Big fans.*

[Silence . . .]

Sir Adam: *We think you could really add . . .*

[Click . . .]

So welcome to ~~Sabu's~~ Johnny Grunge's master class: Table Breaking 101.

Johnny Grunge, Opening Statement:

It's just like if you throw a curveball, if you know what you're doing, you gotta kind of master it, 'til you know what you're doing. There's a right way and the wrong way, just like everything.

Johnny Grunge's Five Simple Steps to Breaking a Table

1. "Just hit it right."
2. "You actually want to break the table yourself."
3. "You don't want to land on the person — you're 250, 300 pounds coming down on an eight foot banquet table."
4. "The longer something is, I mean, science will prove, the longer it is, the weaker it is in the middle."
5. "I mean, that's science . . . you hit it right in the middle, it's gonna break."

PHANTOM

I still don't know how to do it.

SIR ADAM

Me neither, but I'll be happy to try to put you through one now.

After making a name for itself through house shows and video tape sales, ECW eventually signed a TV deal and could be seen around the country.

Bobby Eaton: I agree that it was exciting. And I agree that people want to see you cut your head off, put barbed wire up your ass.

Larry Zbyszko: All I heard was people were hitting people with hammers in the audience . . . I found no reason to stay up and watch.

It wasn't exactly hammers, but many fans around the country were staying up and watching ECW, which aired in some areas as late as 3 a.m. So while Larry was sleeping, ECW was producing some of the most exciting hours in wrestling history.

PHANTOM

One night in my single guy days, I was at a bar with some friends. Things didn't go well with the ladies that night, and it looked like good old Phantom was going home alone once again. In my drunken stupor, I glanced up at a TV in the bar, and noticed something I had never seen before. It was wrestling, but during the match a fan handed Tommy Dreamer a frying pan. And he used it, smashing Raven over the head. After I saw that, I was hooked.

Tod Gordon: It was *The Rocky Horror Picture Show*. The fans brought their own weapons. I mean, up until the point it got carried away and we had to start confiscating them. They had their own songs and chants that went along with each person. It was give and take — it was interactive.

Jim Cornette (From a 3/97 *GIR Radio* Interview)**:** Sure they have a cult following. So does *The Rocky Horror Picture Show*. I don't think they bumped *Star Wars* off a lot of screens last week. I don't like what they did. I don't think it resembles wrestling. It makes me ashamed to be a part of the sport, to see some of the things that they [aired] on their television.

SIR ADAM

> I actually liked the time slot: 2 AM on Saturday nights. It gave me and Phantom just enough time to go out and get drunk and then, just before we'd succumb to alcohol poisoning, watch wrestling. And not just any wrestling — a show where every match was packed with excitement, unbelievable high spots, great drama and women that looked like porn stars. Actually, those were the same things we were out looking for on a Saturday night in the first place.

Tod Gordon: Paul Heyman basically lived in the studio. He made people who had bad matches look like they had good matches. He had people who had average to good matches look like they had incredible matches. He knew when to take a spot out and leave a spot in. He knew what music to put to a video, he had his finger on the pulse of the music industry, incredibly, at that time. I give him full, complete credit for that. He was an eccentric genius.

> In 1995, while ECW's television show was getting rave reviews from wrestling fans all around the United States, something occurred in WCW that would help take the upstart promotion to the next level. At that time, a mid-card wrestler named Steve Austin was being fired — over the phone — by his boss, Eric Bischoff.

Stone Cold with mullet and tiger pants

Steve Austin (From a 9/97 *GIR Radio* Interview): After wcw fired me over the phone — as only a coward would do — I knocked all the hair off and went to being exactly what I am. I got frustrated and pissed off about the situation in wcw. And I finally had something that I could actually talk about and channel into an interview. So ecw was the outlet. Did I know I had that ability? I knew I could do it, but I finally got the chance to do it.

Paul Heyman gave Steve Austin the forum to create news-making promos running down his former employer, Eric Bischoff, as well as Hulk Hogan, or anyone else he wanted to talk about. Austin was putting the spotlight on himself, but also on ecw as well. In his short stint in the company, Austin managed to help get notoriety for ecw, while getting himself a wwf contract at the same time. The rest is Stone Cold history.

Steve Austin (From a 9/97 *GIR Radio* Interview): Paul E gave me a shot there when my arm was still hurt, and all I did was interviews. Paul E was good to me.

Whether it's positive or negative, the name of the former boss of ecw, Paul Heyman, elicits a response from everyone in the wrestling business.

PHANTOM

Heyman is one of the big three in a *Get in the Ring* interview. We always ask: "What do you think of Paul Heyman, Vince McMahon and Eric Bischoff?"

SIR ADAM

If a guest starts to rip on any of the big three, you can be sure it will be a good interview. It just proves further that Paul Heyman really made an impact.

Jake Roberts: Paul E? I don't like him anymore — he abused people, man. When you have kids doing the stupid shit he had them doing, for a damn job, in the hope that you might get a big break, that ain't right, brother.

Diamond Dallas Page: He was the fucking mad scientist, you know, that tooled all the shit together, tweaked all the buttons.

Johnny Grunge: When Paul Heyman approached me, I was in the Philippines doing a seven day tour. He flew all the way over there just to talk to Teddy and me. I remember sitting in a room talking to him and then hearing a bunch of commotion. While he was in there talking to us, a couple of rooms down, he had his suit hanging in his bathroom with the shower running so it would steam the wrinkles out, because he was going to manage that night [as Paul E. Dangerously]. And he forgot to pull the plug in the tub, so he was flooding the nicest hotel in the Philippines — the whole floor!

Jim Cornette (From a 3/97 *GIR Radio* Interview): Paul E. Dangerously, there's no love lost between me and him. The only two things he's ever been able to beat me at: he lost his hair before I did and his waist got to forty before mine.

Despite Jim Cornette's contempt for Heyman and everything ECW related, the WWF and WCW were taking notice. They saw the growing fan interest in this relatively small promotion and began to change their styles to match what was going on in Philadelphia.

Diamond Dallas Page: I was the first guy in WCW to do it, with Savage. We'd fight through the crowd. I got that from ECW. They were fighting everywhere. They made it original — I made it an art form. Where they used garbage cans, I used props, fucking sets. At Halloween Havoc, when Benoit threw me through the sign, I choreographed all that shit . . .

Sean Waltman: I remember when ECW was still in business and you'd talk to Pat Patterson; he'd complain, "This shit they're doing, it's hurting the business." But six months later, guess what? Guess what's happening on WWF TV? Hardcore Title matches, people beating the shit out of each other with chairs, you know? All that stuff. I mean, think about it. No one promotion influenced the entire business like ECW.

> While the blood was flowing and the fans were cheering, there was a growing concern in the business about the violent style ECW was responsible for introducing to the mainstream fan.

Bill Apter: They were always raising the bar in ECW. Going through a flaming table wasn't enough — they had to top that the next night. I was wondering if someone was going to do a snuff wrestling match eventually.

Ken Shamrock: Heyman captured backyard wrestling on TV. He followed different angles than the WWF and WCW, and he went totally extreme. I mean, he went to ten tables, jumping off the top of a balcony, smashing cans on people's heads and cutting them.

Dave Meltzer: Before, you could do one decent chair shot — you didn't have to kill the guy's brains, and you could use it for a finish. You could use it for juice or you could use it for whatever. And then when people saw people take one after the other of those scary, really bad chair shots and stay on their feet, that made it really hard. It's very [tough] on the wrestlers and the promoters and the writers because the audience has seen so much.

> There is some debate amongst the ECW crew as to whether all this violence was really necessary, and whether it was a style that disregarded the mat psychology to which the sport has always adhered.

Shane Douglas: In ECW I think a lot of people subscribed to the idea that if the fans weren't chanting "ECW" every second of the match, then the match was boring. So guys would get up and slam each other with broken chairs, broken tables, or pull razorblades, that kind of stuff.

Justin Credible: We definitely were breaking new ground with the things we were doing, but to say there was no psychology? There certainly was psychology. It may have been a different psychology, but it was there. Tommy Dreamer's actually very underrated, and he taught me a lot of psychology.

> As the years went on, the "ECW style" influenced American wrestling to a point where wrestlers were going out night after night, trying to top each other with more outrageous high spots. A hardcore division soon popped up in the WWF, and WCW employed a more stunt-oriented style. However, old school wrestling fans started clamoring for the return of ring psychology. In other words, they wanted the moves to mean more rather than just being a stunning visual display.

Diamond Dallas Page: I'll give you the best example. *Die Hard*. The first one is unbelievable. But by the third one, there were so many explosions I was going, "Okay, stop the movie right here." We're half way through and this could be a good movie, but they keep blowing shit up. That's what happened with ECW.

Tod Gordon: I think when we became aware of that fact, we tried to go a different direction. I mean, we always tried to have a different mixture of all different types of bouts on the card, but when we realized that, yes, people had gotten anesthetized to multiple chair shot, we knew that we had to reeducate them a bit. That's where the Rey Mysterio/Psychosis matches or the Juventud Guerrera matches or the Guerrero/Benoit/Malenko series came from.

> Gordon and Heyman started to feature more of a wrestling style in the product, but for every Dean Malenko/Eddie Guerrero classic that was embraced by the fans, there was a Shane Douglas/Tully Blanchard scientific match that the ECW crowd turned on. ECW realized that things like barbed wire and tables were their bread and butter. As a result, they would always be prominently featured in one form or another. And no matter what style the respective wrestlers utilized in ECW, there was a family-like feeling in the ECW locker room.

Johnny Grunge: There's never going to be a locker room, ever, probably in the history of this business, like there was in ECW. It was a group of guys who weren't trying to stab each other in the back. It was a group there. We said, "Hey, were all in this together, let's make it work, we got something." I didn't care if I had to put you over. You didn't care about if you're the main event or not. I mean, hell, we had tag teams for the main event for how many years? It was unheard of having a tag team match for the main event. But it didn't bother the heavyweight champion. It didn't bother us. We said, "Let us go on first."

Jerry Lynn: You knew every time you came to work you were going to be thoroughly entertained — and that was just by the boys on the crew.

Rob Van Dam (From a 10/03 *GIR Radio* Interview): All the ECW guys are super tight.

SIR ADAM

Our first experience watching ECW live was at the Elks Lodge in Queens, New York. It was accurately nicknamed "The Madhouse of Extreme." The Queens location became something of a second home for ECW.

PHANTOM

It must have been 150 degrees in that place. I had a hard time concentrating on the matches because I was sweating so damn much. The other fans didn't seem to mind, but damn, there was no air flow.

SIR ADAM

We waited by the locker room and tried to get interviews with the guys. We got to talk to D-Von Dudley, Justin Credible and Spike Dudley, but we hung around for a while and waited for Rob Van Dam. As a fan, the ECW version of RVD is still my favorite wrestler of all time. Anyway, the guys were really just hanging around in the dressing room, talking. So we stood outside with our tape recorder.

PHANTOM

This was long after the matches were over and no one was taking off. It really did look like the entire roster really got along well. We finally spotted RVD and he made a beeline for this other guy with a tape recorder. We were scooped!

SIR ADAM

Who was this idiot, you may be thinking? Another wrestling show? I can tell you that RVD looked ecstatic to talk to him.

PHANTOM

It was a reporter from *High Times* magazine. A crew member told us RVD was waiting for the guy all night.

Rob Van Dam (From a 10/03 *GIR Radio* Interview)**:** That's where the RVD 4:20 started, in Queens. That's where the ball started rolling, guys.

SIR ADAM

We waited for an hour, hoping to get Rob when he was done with *High Times*. But they talked forever, and it didn't seem like they were ever going to finish . . .

PHANTOM

That has always been our downfall. We tire easily. Other wrestling fanatics probably would have waited four hours, but we decided to go eat instead.

SIR ADAM

So we drove off. But we encountered something bizarre, something we were finally able to discuss with Bam Bam Bigelow in March 2002.

Phantom: Bam Bam, you are a normal guy — we met you on the street after an ECW card, Madhouse of Extreme, in Queens. We saw you picking up about fifteen mangos from a deli.

Sir Adam: This idiot, Phantom, got us lost. And we pulled over to a deli to ask for directions.

Bam Bam Bigelow: I remember that.

Phantom: We said, "How can you eat so many?" And you said, "I love mangos."

Bam Bam Bigelow: Heh-heh. In Queens, you don't want to eat nothing, you don't want to drink the water, you know what I mean?

PHANTOM

In one night we learned that RVD loved horticulture and that Bam Bam Bigelow loved mangos. And I got heat stroke from the Madhouse of Extreme.

SIR ADAM

After our experience in Queens, we always believed that the guys in ECW were a tightly knit group.

PHANTOM

Even before that night, when we'd set up an interview with Tazz, Bubba Ray Dudley would confirm the interview. When we'd call the ECW offices in Philadelphia, Steven Richards would answer the phone. It was like everyone had a job other than just going out there and wrestling. It helped to bring them closer together.

SIR ADAM

All that changed in August 2003, when New Jack appeared on *Get in the Ring*. Our sense of the ECW family was shattered forever.

New Jack (From an 8/03 *GIR Radio* Interview)**:** I heard you talking about the Blue Meanie, Blue Meanie is a punk. I hate the Blue Meanie. I hate that cocksucker.

PHANTOM

When New Jack came back on the show in January 2004, we were happy. Maybe he wanted to take back what he said about his family member — maybe, the last time, he was just having a bad day.

New Jack (From an 1/04 *GIR Radio* Interview): D-Von and Bubba bit off of everybody in ECW with a combination of everybody's stuff and then they went to Vince [McMahon] like they had this new idea. And all of a sudden, they the Dudley New Jack. Ain't nothing original about D-Von and Bubba. And they was trying to call me out on the radio, bro. This ain't no promotional thing. What's going to happen is D-Von is going get out of his car one night and New Jack is going to be standing there looking at him. Me and Bubba got in a fight one night. It was at a building in Reading, a fan had attacked Balls Mahoney. We went out there and we had to fight him. Bubba was out there fighting like a girl. Dude, Bubba dropped his head and started swinging his arms like a windmill. That's when I knew. I said, "Bubba, you're the last person in the world I want to be in a bar with getting in a fight." Paul Heyman knows I don't like him. And I'd whip his ass to Japan if I ever saw him.

SIR ADAM

Remind me to send New Jack a Christmas card this year.

PHANTOM

In doing more interviews for the book, we learned that, at times, the ECW locker room could be just as political, with as much backstabbing as any other locker room.

Shane Douglas: What started to happen was a whole lot of copy-catism. Each [guy] had a niche gimmick — mine was talking, Sabu's was breaking tables, Tazz was the shooter. Everybody had their own little niche, at least in the early days, and then what happened was after Sabu started breaking tables, Public Enemy came in and copied it. Then suddenly everyone got on the microphone and started using the "F" word, and then suddenly everyone was swinging chairs or a stick like Sandman.

Tod Gordon: I think that Shane is very bitter, has always been very bitter. He was bitter about WCW, he was bitter about WWF, he was bitter about ECW — and I'm sure someday he'll be bitter about TNA. That's Shane's personality, he's a bitter guy.

Rob Van Dam (From a 10/03 *GIR Radio* Interview)**:** We all had to make a lot of adjustments coming in to WWE from ECW, and obviously a lot of guys couldn't make the adjustments.

> RVD's comment brings up an interesting point. Although most of ECW's top stars went on to careers in WWE and WCW, very few of them ever reached the heights they achieved under Paul Heyman's guidance. For every Rob Van Dam or Chris Benoit there are plenty of Tommy Dreamers, Rhynos, Public Enemys and Justin Credibles. Was it the wrestlers themselves who couldn't make the transition, or was it something else?

SIR ADAM

> There's no denying that most of the ECW guys weren't as tall or as physically imposing as the typical WWE wrestler.

Kevin Kelly: When Tazz came out at MSG and heard that electrifying roar, with just the heartbeat of his music, that said that ECW had made an impact on the wrestling business. That would be the single greatest moment in ECW history, in my mind — when Tazz appeared at the Garden.

PHANTOM

It might have been an amazing moment, but all Sir Adam and I could talk about was how small Tazz looked. Whether it was because of the difference between the size and scope of the ECW Arena and Madison Square Garden or that Tazz just shrunk in the months after his last ECW appearance, I don't know.

SIR ADAM

He shrunk?

PHANTOM

You're telling me your grandparents didn't shrink?

SIR ADAM

Yeah, but they were eighty.

PHANTOM

That's the only thing I can think of — I was so scared of Tazz in ECW, but at the Royal Rumble it looked like he was shorter than me.

SIR ADAM

He is shorter than you, but that was part of the magic of ECW. Yes, many of these guys were dwarfed when they reached WCW or the WWF, and it was something that Paul Heyman was cognizant of and used to his advantage. On our show, whenever Paul Heyman's name is mentioned, nine times out of ten the wrestler ends up saying something like this . . .

Perry Saturn (From an 11/02 *GIR Radio* Interview): Paul E is phenomenal . . . He's unbelievable. He hides your weaknesses and gets your strong points out. You had guys that were superstars in ECW who went somewhere else and just didn't make it.

PHANTOM

Why would you try to sneak in a Saturn quote?

SIR ADAM

Because the second time he was on the show (on the phone, of course) he was a lot more cordial. And because it's always fun to see you freak out whenever his name is mentioned.

Justin Credible: Paul's biggest strength as a promoter and a booker was to really pull out our strengths and hide our weaknesses. He'd manipulate us the way he wanted us to be and utilize us all to his advantage and to the promotion's advantage. He brought out a confidence I never had — that I could be that main event level guy that I never dreamed of being.

Paul Heyman addresses the troops

Shane Douglas: He put together a group of talent that was incredible and underexposed. Each of us had our strengths and Paul saw what nobody else did. Who would have ever thought that Shane Douglas, in 1993, would be one of the hottest heels in the business? At that time heels had to be fat, with a wart on their face and a beer gut. Paul was one of the few that said, "This guy can be a natural heel, let him go with it." What [he] didn't do was have someone go out there and cut promos on Tazz about how short he was. Nobody came out there and said Shane Douglas can't do a moonsault . . .

Prior to the time he sold his stake in ECW to Paul Heyman, rumors were rampant that Tod Gordon was actually helping WCW sign away ECW's talent pool. While Heyman wanted to hold on to as much talent as he possibly could, Gordon had a different philosophy: that the ECW brand was what sold tickets, and that everyone was replaceable.

Tod Gordon: Paul and I disagreed so much when Public Enemy left. He felt crushed by it, believing it was a terrible thing they did. And meanwhile, I'm helping them move on. I was the one who called Kevin Sullivan and tried to get them a better deal than Vince was giving them — which they got. I said, these guys busted their asses for me, don't get mad because their taking $150,000 and I'm giving them $50,000. They're my friends, they tried to help me make money, more power to them.

By late 1997, Tod Gordon had officially split from ECW. He saw the writing on the wall. He knew the company was in deep trouble.

Tod Gordon: It had become so much more of a business than pleasure — meaning more things were going on than just sitting there and creating angles. So many details were bogging down our day—things that were not Paul's strong suit — that, unfortunately, we were less and less able to focus on the product itself.

The exodus of talent to WCW *did* damage ECW, no matter what Tod Gordon believed. ECW hadn't become established as the kind of brand name that could survive without the performers fans came to know and love. One veteran wrestler who had gained power as booker of wcw saw what was happening in ecw and was licking his chops at the thought of recreating that feeling for Ted Turner.

Kevin Sullivan: ECW was Florida Championship Wrestling taken to another level. If you look at it, Paul E. was a great student. He was around a lot of guys at the right time in their career. And if you look at the Florida Championship era in the '80s it wasn't much different.

Tod Gordon: Kevin Sullivan went to WCW and in a short period of time pretty much took a third of our talent. He took Benoit, Malenko, Guerrero; he took the Mexicans; he took Konnan and Rey Mysterio. Basically, he just raided us.

Even Terry Funk noticed the changes at wcw as ecw talents were being raided.

Terry Funk (From an 8/96 *GIR Radio* Interview): Look at Turner. He said, "I don't want violence on TV." But what has been the turn of WCW? It's been towards violence in the last six months. Believe me, the other companies watch ECW like hawks.

PHANTOM

It's almost like that time when Sonny Ono tried to buy us out of our exclusive contract with WGBB. He wanted to make us a Japanese wrestling show, but we held our ground.

SIR ADAM

What are you talking about? You were begging him to buy us out, you even started taking Japanese at Nassau Community College.

PHANTOM

Oh yeah. I guess I would have sold out too. *Konichiwa*.

To the wrestling fan it looked like things couldn't have been going better for ECW. After Barely Legal in April 1997, they were producing bi-monthly Pay-per-view events. But many people we spoke to point to this as the time when ECW started to sink — under the pressures of having a leader that couldn't say "No" to his wrestlers, and under massive debts.

Jerry Lynn: One night I had a two out of three falls match with Justin Credible at the ECW arena. I told Justin that night, "We're not gonna ask permission to do anything. We're just gonna go out there and do what we do." So we went out and we tore the house down. And we went in the back and you could tell there were certain guys who weren't happy.

Rob Van Dam (From a 10/03 *GIR Radio* Interview)**:** In ECW, we didn't have those stiff perimeters. You could go out, if you were the first or second match on the card, and you could try to steal the show: don't worry about keeping it down, saving it for the rest of the card. You could go out and do everything in the book. I'd be walking through the curtain for a Pay-per-view, and Paul Heyman would say to me: "Go out there and steal the show." He didn't care if I'd go out there for five minutes, twenty minutes, it was up to me. If I was going to fight in the crowd, bring a chair in, if I was going to set a table up, it was all up to me.

Shane Douglas: I used to tell him, "Damn, Paul, you're the boss. Only you can tell these guys not to do it." Heyman wanted to be the boss so damn badly he tasted it. He wanted it, but then you'd come to him and say, "Paul, you gotta tell these guys to stop doing this." But that was nowhere near what he was going to say or do.

As time passed, Heyman started to fall behind financially, owing more and more of his workers money. For many, bad feelings still remain. Conspiracy theorists point fingers, insinuating that Heyman jumped off a sinking ECW ship long before the fateful day in 2001 when the company was officially no more.

Shane Douglas: Acclaim Video walked away with an incredibly sweet deal — they had to pay no royalties or anything on the ECW video game. They came in and used what we had built and paid a small stipend to ECW . . . Paul was a maniac as a businessman. He gave something away that was very, very valuable — and got nothing in return for it except a little bit of exposure. Well, guess what? Exposure don't pay the bills.

Kevin Kelly: Vince McMahon was paying Paul Heyman a thousand dollars a week from 1996 on . . . He had a financial stake in ECW. Paul started working for the company in a consultant role. When they shot the opening for Shotgun Saturday Night all around the city of New York, Paul was helping find locations. So while Paul was telling his boys that Vince and them were the enemy, and as he was telling his fan base that Vince and them were the enemy, he was on the payroll the whole time.

New Jack (From a 1/04 *GIR Radio* Interview)**:** Paul E. left ECW owing everybody money. The deal when he came to WWF was this: if y'all sign off the money I owe you, I'll give you a contract. So, with all the money he owed everyone, they had to sign a release saying he don't owe them no more.

> In the end there was no huge sendoff — ECW ended with a whimper. But as a federation that existed for only nine years, making such an impact on the industry means ECW was something special. Not only for the fans, but for its wrestlers as well.

Chris Candido: It was definitely the best for me — until the end. A lot of the boys, like myself, ended up losing a lot of money, having to sell your house and stuff like that. If you can still say it was the best time in your life even after you had to sell everything you owned then it must've been the best.

Vic Grimes: ECW was the best promotion. I truly believe that they worked harder than any other wrestlers in the business. I believe they bumped harder. I believe they tried harder. It was all about

Vic Grimes trying to unload some T-shirts

giving 120 percent instead of just collecting a paycheck. It was about showing people what you could actually do instead of going through the motions.

EC LON

EC DUB! EC DUB! EC DUB!

Chapter 7

Has the Internet Ruined Wrestling?

Viscera: It's just too much information. I mean, wrestling used to be all about mystery. Now, they've taken that away.

At first glance the Internet seems like a die-hard wrestling fan's dream come true. An endless array of information, a place to share ideas and thoughts with fellow fans and a way to keep tabs on wrestling going on in other parts of the world. And for many people it is just that. Certain fans, however, instead of being smartened up, becoming more dedicated to the product, have actually become jaded. Essentially, wrestling comes down to the suspension of disbelief, the ability to get caught up in the moment, and for some the Internet has destroyed that. Even more disturbing, most wrestling sites have begun to read like supermarket tabloids. Who's dating who; who's being reprimanded backstage; who crapped in someone else's lunch as a rib — that kind of thing. It's something not lost on the wrestlers.

Buff Bagwell: I can't step out of my house and fart without reading,

Who, me? I didn't fart

"Oh God, Buff was there and he farted." I don't know how the hell they find out, but it's like there's cameras on every street in the world. It's the weirdest damn thing.

If you search the Net for wrestling sites, you'll find message boards filled with criticism, news sites chock full of information on wrestlers' personal lives and, generally, a negative attitude towards the sport itself. This has even been carrying over into the arenas. Today, a slip while climbing the turnbuckles results in an instantaneous chant of "You fucked up." In our opinion, it's something that threatens to become a prominent part of the business.

SIR ADAM

I'm not above this. I'll admit it — I love this stuff. But I also think it's compromising my love for the business. And I'm concerned.

PHANTOM

Are you kidding me? I loved hearing how Teddy Hart and CM Punk got into a fight outside the White Irash Café in Nashville, Tennessee. It increases my love for the sport. Now I know these two legitimately hate each other.

SIR ADAM

You're such a gossip. This is a serious problem which needs to be examined. Let's get to work.

Chris Candido: I think the Internet totally fucked us up. The fans get a lot more information — not necessarily what they shouldn't know — but it's harder to make angles work. I mean, it's fine when people start knowing things, but at the same time there's just way too much stuff out there.

Jerry Lynn: If you don't like the Internet don't read it.

Jerry makes a good point, but it's hard to resist when all the questions you ever had can be answered with just a few quick searches. The extent of what's available online is unbelievable. Many of the wrestlers themselves feel compelled to read the Internet for the latest news. It's just human nature.

Rob Van Dam (From a 10/19/03 *GIR Radio* Interview): I don't put anything into the websites and the different reports, because a lot of times they're so far off they're ridiculous. And some times, we're human, sometimes you can't help but actually develop feelings. At least me, myself, I'm not above that, actually developing feelings for somebody that writes something that's an absolutely ridiculous lie.

Jeff Hardy (From a 3/03 *GIR Radio* Interview): The Internet, oh my God, there's so much crap on there that's just not true. It's amazing how many things people just automatically believe. I don't know how many times I've seen, on different websites, that I have chronic fatigue syndrome or some other craziness. It's just so untrue. I just let it go. It's like I'm kind of giving in if I even write anything. I mean, I want to, all the time, and I just never do. Matt's [online] a lot, as soon as he gets in a hotel room, he's looking for an outlet to plug in. He lets that stuff get to him.

Bobby Eaton: Everybody's a wrestling fan in this business. I don't give a damn what they say.

> To many wrestlers, the problem is not just that the information is often false, it's that the fans can be extremely vicious. It's like these type of fans are not happy unless they complain. Another part of the problem? On the Internet it's far too easy to be anonymous. If you have a computer and some time on your hands you can start up your own news site or radio program and, instantly, people think you're an expert.

PHANTOM

Isn't that what we did?

SIR ADAM

Yes, but I think ever since you admitted you don't really wear a mask we've been accepted more.

Chris Candido: You know, earlier when it was just guys like Dave Meltzer and Wade Keller writing their things — at least those guys had an in when it was just them. But when a fourteen year old kid can write, "Hey, Bret Hart's gay . . . " It annoys the hell out of everybody.

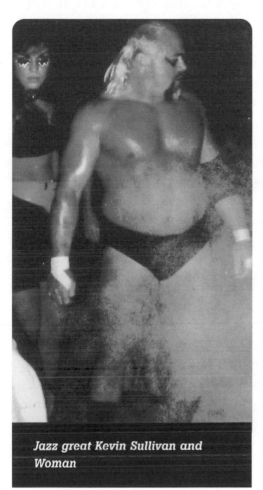

Jazz great Kevin Sullivan and Woman

Kevin Sullivan: I think that a lot of the fans forget this isn't Olivier doing Hamlet — this is Monty Python doing the silly walk. They make it too serious, they break down every move. I don't begrudge them for that, and I see where they're coming from, but I think because of it wrestling became more choreographed . . . Guys with sheets of paper for every move they were going to do, I always thought that good pro wrestling was jazz. I think it's jazz, good jazz.

It seems crazy, but certain wrestlers have changed their in-ring style to appease this part of the audience. Still, the majority maintain that if you haven't walked a mile in their boots, you should just shut the hell up.

Shane Douglas: First of all, one of the things I just cannot stand are people who Monday morning quarterback. Never had a pair of boots on in their life, never been in the ring working when a muscle ripped, a bone broke or a knee blew, whatever — but they're going to sit there and offer up what you did wrong in your match and how they could've done it better.

Jake Roberts: Let me ask you a question. How can you respect someone's opinion about wrestling when they've never wrestled?

> Of course, we disagree with Jake. If we didn't, we would never have been able to do our show. Although we've never wrestled, we have been astute fans of the business since we were children and we know what we like and don't like. Just because we never directed a movie we can still say that *Santa with Muscles* sucked. Any fan should be able to voice their opinion — but what we're talking about in this chapter is more than just criticism, it's that part of the audience who actually seem to *hate* what they're paying to see.

Erik Watts: In the last twelve years I haven't found an Internet site that's ever said anything less than they wished I would die.

> Okay, even Erik will tell you that he's not in the same league as a Chris Benoit, but is he really as bad as everyone claims? If you're unfamiliar with how critics assess Watts' in-ring skills, consider how he himself describes a recent Internet recap of a show he was on.

Erik Watts: They must have done five paragraphs of what was exciting about the show — the only thing that sucked about the show was me. I'm thinking to myself, you called the show mediocre, you gave it five good segments, and you mean to tell me that I am the equivalent? I pulled down five good segments? I suck that bad?

> Wrestling has always featured many different styles. Some wrestlers are more athletic than others; some are more technically sound; and some more physical. We could go on and on, but the bottom line is it takes a little bit of everything to make a great show. Most Internet critics favor what can best described as a "work-oriented" style — those who don't perform that way, to them, are useless.

Erik Watts: It's like they've got their rules of thumb. You don't push around Flair. You don't push around Funk. And then there's the circle of people that they can beat up all the time. To me, it's like cheap heat. Hell, if you're an Internet writer and you want to make sure you please your peers, just throw in Erik Watts sucks and no matter how bad your article's been, they all think you're a pretty good writer because they all agree. To me it's a joke. And then to listen to some of these guys ideas and how pathetic they are . . .

> Another part of the problem is that the Internet has become almost monolithic, the be-all and end-all domain of "smart marks" — the place where all of wrestling's "problems" (everything from awkward storylines and uninspired booking to financial tribulations and general public perception) are solved. Good sites and bad sites are lumped together under one banner: "The Internet." It's so easy to do, in fact, that we're guilty of it here. But it's not like talking about "The Newspaper." When talking about hard news, few people are going to assume you mean *The Syosset High School Tribune*.

Wade Keller (Editor & Publisher, *Pro Wrestling Torch*): The Internet . . . when people say it with a certain tone . . . it's kind of the same thing people are trying to communicate when they say "dirt sheets" or "rag sheets." They're demeaning a certain element of it . . . I'm proud of what I do and I know that I have that I have gone through journalism school, I've gone through internships at news stations, I've seen how journalism works and I think that I live up to or exceed the standards of journalism.

Dave Meltzer (Editor & Publisher, *Wrestling Observer*): People group a lot of them — it all has the same value. And the fact is that there are some sites that I see stuff on and they're right half the time, a third of the time — and they're wrong a lot. Some sites are pretty accurate — but people don't know the difference. So a lot of inaccurate stuff gets around pretty quick.

> Whether or not fans can tell the difference between legitimate news sites and more untrustworthy sources, the fact remains that everyone is reading this stuff. Right? At least that's what we

thought. The prevailing opinion within the industry is that hardcore Internet fans are really a small percentage of the audience — no matter how vocal they may sometimes be.

Chris Kanyon: To this day, I don't see the hardcore fans amounting to much. At the most, ten percent of our audience on a Monday night.

Scott Hudson: So many of the writers and bookers try to cater to ten percent of the audience rather than letting the ninety percent dictate what they should be doing. They're catering to the smallest common denominator, instead of appealing to the masses.

Shane Douglas: Yeah, I think sometimes ECW and WCW worried too much about it. The Internet is perhaps thousands of fans, but I think it's a clear minority of the fans that watch our shows.

SIR ADAM

This is something that has always baffled me. Shouldn't you be most loyal to your hardcore fans?

For some promoters, the Internet is often a valuable and powerful marketing tool. It allows them to reach their target audience in a quick, cost-effective manner. To these guys, Internet fans are treated like royalty.

Jeff Jarrett: People can dive into tnawrestling.com and learn a whole lot about our promotion at their schedule, at their time. You don't have to wait until the TV show comes on.

Industry observers will tell you that wwe, however, is not as concerned about catering to hardcore Internet fans. Their belief? Those fans will always be there.

Wade Keller: From talking to people who are still in WWE the feeling I get is that there's been kind of a rebellion against paying attention to it — unless something presents itself that really commands attention. It got so negative that the people with the most power in WWE don't want it brought up all that often. I also think they came to the realization that the percentage of people who are really on the Internet sites five times a week, or ten times a week or ten times a day, is so small that they didn't need to put in a lot of resources worrying about what was said.

Dave Meltzer: The rank and file television viewer . . . will go to wrestling when it's really, really hot. Those people aren't spending their time on wrestling websites. The super hardcore fans, of course they are — but they're the super hardcore fans . . . It's such a minor part of the big picture that it could have a small effect one way or the other, but it couldn't have a big effect one way or the other.

Kevin Kelly: I think the Internet is extremely overrated in how it has affected wrestling, because the Internet does not sell tickets to wrestling. The Internet does not drive the casual fan, which is how you really change the wrestling business. The same core audience that looks at the Internet are also the ones who will consistently watch a wrestling product. The same core, the same niche, they're going to be there regardless . . . The Internet doesn't expand the audience.

Sean Waltman: It's the die hard fans that are going to watch every week anyhow — even when it sucks.

SIR ADAM

I'm starting to realize that wrestling and I have a very unhealthy relationship. All the signs say we should break up — but they keep making me think things will get better again. Like they were in the beginning. Those were good times.

PHANTOM

In the last two years, WWE has flat out told us that they would rather have their employees go on mainstream shows than one, like ours, that targets a smaller, hardcore audience. How they can honestly think that they can convince a bunch of old women watching *The View* to order Judgment Day is beyond me. However, I'll guarantee you that a good GIR interview with Kane will result in many fans who were on the ledge about spending $30 for a Pay-per-view to buy the show.

SIR ADAM

I see your point, but for entertainment value alone, I'd pay $30 to see Kane chokeslam Star Jones.

WWE's attitude toward hardcore fans is a far cry from what it was during the Monday night wars. Back then, WCW would agonize over its decisions in an attempt to outsmart the "smarts." Wrestling fans love surprises and *Nitro* attempted to play up to that. What got lost in the shuffle is that most of WCW's fans didn't read the Internet as closely as we do, and didn't understand many of the insider comments. What made WCW so big at the time was that they had been able to harness the mainstream audience, the hardcore fans were just along for the ride.

Dave Meltzer: On *Nitro*, when they used to do those Internet comments, and you'd listen to the audience — this was when *Nitro* was hot, they were actually drawing a lot of people — you'd just hear those comments just die. The reality is that if that is your number one source of fans then you're dead anyway because you can't make a profit, there's not enough people.

Rick Steiner: In WCW, that is one of things they always tried to do: "Let's try to fool the sheets, let's try to kayfabe it so no one knows." It was one of those things we always had to worry about.

Buff Bagwell: Going to *Nitro* and stuff, we're on a private jet, so the bookers always talked about the Internet. Internet? I'm thinking,

"What the hell?" So they actually got so outlandish with it that they started talking about reversing everything that was on the Internet to shock people.

Wade Keller: I think that during the Monday night wars both companies were very concerned about how they were seen by the Internet because it was so new. I don't think they had a real idea of the scope, of how much of their audience was seeing it. Really, it used to be, "The dirt sheets? It's only a few thousand people who read them, and in any arena we go to it might be two or three people." The Internet was available to everyone, on any computer in any house, in any workplace, in any library. And that scared promoters and old time wrestlers who'd been around a while — because it was so accessible. I think there was almost a paranoia about it at first. As things settled, the companies said, "You know what? If we ignore them, and go about our business, we might have a little less aggravation."

PHANTOM

I've never bought the argument that the Internet fan base is so small. If you like something, why wouldn't you want to learn more about it on the Internet? I like garlic, so I am often on sites that have to do with the intricacies and different ways to use that delectable spice. For instance, did you know that in 1641 Charles Von Garlic . . .

SIR ADAM

As your friend I'm urging you to stop right now. We get the point. You don't have to let the world know about your spice fetish.

Triple H may call himself "The Game," but for many wrestling fans, figuring out the surprises before they happen is the real game — and the Internet made the game a little easier. In some cases, it actually ruined the fun. Today, wrestling promoters have essentially lost the ability to tape shows in advance. *Smackdown* results, for example, are available online — often just minutes after the live event ends. It's undeniable — spoilers have an effect on fan enthusiasm.

A.J. Styles: I would say it has spoiled wrestling fans a little bit, because now they're not going to take the time to watch a match unless they know it's a great match. But people have different perspectives on what a great match is.

SIR ADAM

I remember trying not to read the spoiler for a Brock Lesnar/Kurt Angle iron man match on *Smackdown*. But I couldn't do it. I couldn't wait two miserable days. Then, because I knew what was going to happen, I taped the show and watched it two days later. It was an amazing match, but all I kept thinking was how great it could have been, live, on *Raw*.

What may have been a great surprise or a captivating finish becomes just an interesting read. Why do we do it, when we would never even dream of finding out how a movie ends before going to the theater? It leaves wrestlers scratching their heads.

Jerry Lynn: I just don't understand. I mean, I'm a wrestling fan and when I watch a TV show or a Pay-per-view or something, I don't want to know the results. That would ruin it for me. I don't know why people do it. To me, it would take all of the fun out of it. Maybe, because they know in advance what's going on, they feel more a part of the business . . .

Wade Keller: I think that there's something to be said for wrestling being an ongoing storyline, one that never ends. Everybody, well, not everybody, a lot of people, have a desire to be a step ahead of the average person watching.

Phantom and Sir Adam meet up with Viscera

Viscera: Some people, you know, want to be, as they say, "smart marks." Be a fan and enjoy it as a fan!

The truth is we hardcore fans have always been like this — we just didn't have the outlet to express ourselves. We listened, but could not speak. And more importantly, we didn't know there was a whole cult of us, waiting to gather. In the old days, the WWF would tape three or four weeks worth of television programs at a time. It was more cost effective and allowed angles to be laid out without fear of injury and other unforeseen circumstances.

Wrestling hotlines made a fortune off this. They used to give out TV taping results and booking plans weeks before they aired, and sprinkled in some locker room gossip for good measure. In 1988, rabid fans knew that the Ultimate Warrior was going to win the Intercontinental title over the Honky Tonk Man in record time. All because of Captain Lou Albano's Wrestleline or Rubberband line, whatever the hell he called it.

Blackjack Brown: I am the originator of hotlines. In 1978 when I used to do the wrestling programs for the WWWF, I was right there projecting the future with a phone in my hand. The Internet definitely ruined what I had going.

SIR ADAM

I cannot express to you how angry my father would get at me for calling Captain Lou Albano's wrestling hotline. It was ninety-nine cents a minute and to say that I called a lot would be an understatement. At first I denied making the calls, then I threw out the bills when they arrived. When they shut off our phone he blocked the numbers, but thank God Coach Kurt's wrestling hotline was a local call.

Norman Kleinberg (Sir Adam's father): When I was growing up we played stickball and looked for girls. That's it. Instead, my son called the Captain Lou Albano hotline every day and stuck me with a bill for $300 a month. As you can imagine, I was very proud.

Sir Adam and Phantom ask Captain Lou for their money back

PHANTOM

Basically Sir Adam and I were doing *Get in the Ring Radio*, before we even had a show. When the hotlines became interactive, fans would be able to talk to other fans for something like $50 a minute. Blackjack Brown, the man my dad refers to as "The guy who took $5,000 out of my retirement fund," acted as the moderator to these wrestling discussions. While normal high school freshman were trying to hook up with girls on "party lines," Sir Adam and I called the wrestling hotline for a half hour because we could speak to Jimmy Garvin, live. We laughed our asses off, asking Jimmy some of the stupidest questions imaginable. The only one who wasn't laughing was my dad.

Isidoro Nudelman (Phantom's Father): I grew up in Brazil. I used to play soccer, using a ball we'd make by stuffing an old, dirty sock with newspaper. Needless to say, we had no money. And I come to America to give my son a better life, and this is what he does? Spends $4500 on talking to Jemmy "Jammy" Gervin? As you can imagine, I too was quite proud of this putz.

Chris Kanyon: If they really wanted it, they could've had Meltzer's newsletter back in the '80s. The information was always there. The Internet just made it easier to find.

PHANTOM

Thanks Kanyon. Where were you when I was getting beat with a shoe?

Norman Kleinberg: A shoe? That's a great idea. I just used whatever I could find in the freezer. It sounds cruel, but if you've ever seen a boy after he gets hit with a frozen slice of pizza . . . it helps straighten him out a little bit.

Isidoro Nudelman: I admire your creativity. I thought I was good that time I pie-faced him with a head of lettuce.

SIR ADAM

I wonder why we're obsessed with such a violent sport.

PHANTOM

Now I know why, to this day, I can't eat a salad without crying. I must have blocked that out.

All of this means that it's not all our fault. Okay, maybe the phone bills. But while keeping spoilers under wraps might be impossible, the problem of backstage information being available on the Net is correctable. After all, those in the know are the ones responsible for spilling the beans.

Jeff Jarrett: It is the business structure side that releases the information. You guys, I'm not trying to lump you in, from the reporters' side, if you guys want that information, it's your job to get it. It's up to the wrestler, the business, the office to allow information that is okay to get out, and information that is not okay not to get out. In this business, sometimes, the guys from within work against the system. And that's not productive.

Rick Steiner: Well, I think that Eric Bischoff, when he was running WCW, and some of the guys he had in the office, like Terry Taylor, who were more connected to the Internet . . . I think stuff leaked out sometimes and people started pointing their fingers.

Jerry Lynn: There's a bunch of wrestlers who, the minute they find out what they're doing — they're on the phone with somebody who writes for the Internet.

Kevin Kelly: It was so weird, because everybody always said they knew Paul Heyman was leaking stuff. They knew it. Okay, so why do you keep him around? Why don't you stop him from doing it by either firing him or saying, "Hey, listen Paul, we know you're leaking stuff, knock it off?" Apparently they turned a blind eye to it, but that was one of things that led to him being removed from the *Smackdown* writing position. I know there was at least one occasion where Paul was told to leak something. The first Pay-per-view that Tazz and Michael Cole got to do some of the work on, they did a rehearsal, you could see how the camera shot was gonna go when Tazz and Michael Cole were gonna be introduced, the little hand-shake and all. Well JR was throwing a hissy fit all day. There is no other way to describe it, just extreme immature behavior on his part. And as all of this was going on and everybody in the truck and backstage were able to see all this going on, it was pretty much known at that point that it was going to be leaked out on purpose — to sort of bloody JR a little bit. He was acting like a baby and that story got leaked on purpose.

So why do hardcore fans seek out dirt when it takes away from their enjoyment? The simple answer is these fans want to be a part of the business in some manner.

Erik Watts: Everyone wants to be a wrestler, and the majority of these critics know that they could never be a wrestler. So what can they be? "Oh, *I got a mind for the business.* I'm not dedicated enough. I'm not going to work out. I don't have the

Of course, the Internet isn't for everybody

size. I'm not tough enough. So, what do I have in common with wrestling? Well, I got a good head on my shoulders. That must mean I could be a booker or promoter."

Although Erik's comments are a bit demeaning, he's not just talking about fans, but people in the business as well. In fact, Erik thinks that Jim Ross falls into this category.

Erik Watts: Don't get me wrong, I love Jim Ross. Jim, before he got into wrestling, was a referee, the whole thing. Brother, let me tell you what, if his body type was a wrestler's body type, he would have been in the ring in two seconds. Thank God he didn't. For the sport, thank God he didn't.

PHANTOM

Jim Ross is really getting trashed in this chapter. I guess he shouldn't have gone on every damn show in America — except ours — to promote his cookbook.

SIR ADAM

I've always said that I love being a journalist and never had any desire to try to become a wrestler, but when I really think back to when I first started following wrestling, back when I was five years old, it was the wrestlers that I emulated. I didn't stand by and commentate or review other kids' fights. I wanted to be a wrestler: it was what lead me to break my arm when a Jimmy Snuka leap off my night table went wrong. It was what made me do a King Harley Race head butt off the couch and knock out my sister's baby tooth. It was wrestling that made me climb a set of nearby steps and give a guy a flying bulldog during a street fight in college. Yes, radio was a dream too, but it only started as I got older, became more practical and saw it as an option. Don't get me wrong, I love being a wrestling journalist, but it definitely was my only way to get in on the fun.

For those fans who don't want to spend ten years of their life traveling to a non-paying radio gig, the Internet is a great place to let you feel more like a part of the action. You're participating and not just watching. Others have followed this same path and even made it to television . . .

Scott Hudson: I don't think Mark Madden or I, or Mike Tenay for that matter, would have gotten the break without the exposure of the Internet and the newsletters and whatnot. I would say its because we're fans. We were fans before we were anything else. We were sort of quasi-historians, if not actual historians of the sport, and we had a healthy appreciation for what the men and women did in the ring. And for what the bookers had to come up with. And it wasn't just a money making proposition for us. It wasn't something we did to get exposure. It was just because we loved the sport and we were fans.

Wade Keller: I mean, we're all fans of certain things. We just choose to get into some of them on the Internet, while others we watch casually. There are TV shows I enjoy, but I don't go on the Internet to read about the in-fights with their management and talent. I think people who do seek out the Internet for inside news are such die-hard fans that there's really nothing they can read or find out about that's going to turn them off.

SIR ADAM

What we're trying to point out is that we're all just fans of professional wrestling — from the guys in the ring to the people watching at home and typing away. We're all hooked on this crazy business, for one reason or another, and we shouldn't make it our life's work to criticize every minute detail. At least not to the point that we forget why we started watching in the first place. Besides, there's enough mainstream media exaggerating and being deceptive with wrestling information. Those are the people we should be fighting with, not each other. When we're amongst ourselves we can still cheer, boo, or throw food at the ref. But lighten up a little.

PHANTOM

All right, Sir Adam. We'll all hold hands and sing "We Are the World." We'll make the wrestling world a brighter place for you and me.

SIR ADAM

Don't make me get out the shoe.

Chapter 8

Is Paul Orndorff Dead?

Shane Douglas: When you don't hear a word from a wrestler or a star for a while, people start to wonder: "Well, I haven't seen Paul Orndorff for a couple of months, so he must be dead."

Society is obsessed with fame. It's a statement that is hard to refute when daily television shows like *Access Hollywood* and weekly supermarket tabloids are a cultural staple and generate millions of dollars in revenue each week. If you need more proof, look at what many people are willing to endure on reality shows just to win some cash and maybe have their 15 minutes. *Survivor* and *Fear Factor* are regularly amongst the highest rated programs. Face it, at one time or another, haven't we all dreamt of being famous, signing autographs, and being interviewed on TV? But now, more than ever, along with the glitz and glamour, part of being in the public eye is knowing that from time to time, rumors are going to spread about your love life, your past and, perhaps, much, much more. Wrestling is no different. Except that in Hollywood, the rumor is usually something like: "Hey, I heard Ben Affleck got in Betty White's pants." In wrestling it's: "Hey, I heard that someone bet Sid Vicious that he couldn't keep a squirrel in his pants for sixty seconds. Sid tried it, but the squirrel bit him on the Vicious family jewels and he needed a rabies shot."

But that's just wrestling. What did you expect?

Jerry Lynn: It's amazing what people come up with. I think they're people that have just way too much time on their hands.

Rumors about these two are often true

Joanie "Chyna" Laurer: I heard so many of them. I used to have a computer and now I don't . . . It just got to be too much.

For the most part, wrestling rumors can be broken down into a few categories. First, there are those that are just pure speculation, based on observing something out of the ordinary. This includes the origins of the hole in S.D. Jones' back, and the discolored blotch on Dusty Rhodes' stomach. Over the years, we've heard many about Stevie Ray's distinctive shoulder and back scars. When Stevie was on our radio show in April 2002, he assured us that the markings were not self-induced, or a fraternity brand. One scar was from a knife fight which was wrestling related and the other was from a fall off a motorcycle going eighty miles per hour. Sometimes these types of rumors are easy for us to get to the bottom of.

S.D. Jones: People have always said the craziest things about it. I've never been shot, never been to Vietnam. I was born with a cyst on my back. I was like eight or nine years old when they operated on me.

Dusty Rhodes (From a 1/04 *GIR Radio* interview): Had it since birth. I've always said it looks a little bit like Africa.

> In speaking with our panel of experts, however, we've found that the majority of wrestling rumors start with a small piece of information that is actually true, but then gets exaggerated beyond all recognition.

Buff Bagwell: They get a little bit of a story, and twist it and turn it. A lot of times there's at least a little bit of a truth, but never in my life have I seen all of the truth. It's just amazing.

> Of course, there are some rumors that are so baseless that the only reasonable explanation has to be either jealousy or sheer hatred. It can be professional or personal, but one thing is certain: rumors like this are created with the intention of ruining someone's life.

Jerry Lynn: One that really sticks in my mind is from when I had a broken ankle one time, when I was still in Minneapolis, doing indies. Someone was spreading a rumor around that I started drinking heavily, that I was an alcoholic, and that I was never going to wrestle again.

Chris Candido: Man, I had to be one of the favorites on the Internet for a real, real long time. They had tons and tons of rumors about me. Being from the same household, myself and Tammy Sytch, generated tons of them: about her doing this, me doing that, us doing stuff together . . . making sexual deals with freaking sheep. A lot of the stuff wasn't true. It wasn't a sheep, it was a goat.

Ahmed Johnson (From a 4/02 *GIR Radio* Interview)**:** Bro, like I told you, I heard rumors that I was a pimp in Miami. It's kind of funny, but in the same way it gets on my damn nerves to hear that kind of stuff.

PHANTOM

I read once that Sir Adam was a male prostitute and Ahmed Johnson was his pimp.

SIR ADAM

Bro, like I told you, I heard rumors that I was a ho in Miami. It's kind of funny, but in the same way it gets on my damn nerves to hear that kind of stuff.

Still, a handful of rumors, while disputed by those involved, are actually true.

Sean Waltman: All the bad stuff that you've heard about me, although some of it may have been blown out of proportion, most of it was true.

Yes, welcome to the wonderful world of wrestling rumors. No, we're not talking about being spotted in the latest hotspot with an exotic model, or even getting married after a drunken night out in Las Vegas. Wrestling rumors are consistently depraved, quite often malicious and, with alarming frequency, downright morbid. Which brings us to the strangest category of all wrestling rumors, those of premature death. You see, the old phrase "out of sight, out of mind" simply does not apply to wrestling. In wrestling, it's more like out of sight, well, then you must be dead.

Jimmy Valiant: Oh brother, I die probably five, six times a year. People, they call my wife, Angel, and they hate to tell her. (Sighs.)

"Angel, I'm sorry, but we just heard it, he died."

Ken Shamrock: It's either he's dead, he's in rehab or he got married. Just the other day I got a call from a friend of mine who heard that I got in a car accident and that I died. He called me up and said, "Dude, I was so worried about you." You'll probably hear about twenty of those things, because people don't see me around enough.

Harley Race: It's been on the Internet probably half a dozen different times that I was dead. I was killed in an accident, oh, right at the time that I had the wreck that took me out of the sport.

Ahmed Johnson (From a 4/02 *GIR Radio* Interview): I'm the only dead person I know that can still talk.

Besides the master of the Pearl River Plunge, you can probably think of a dozen other wrestlers that were rumored dead at some point. For a wrestler, a death rumor is almost a demented rite of passage. Their proliferation has become so rampant, sometimes it seems as if everyone in the world has heard them.

SIR ADAM

Finally, I can get this out. It is undeniable that at one time or another, professional wrestling has touched most people's lives. Even if for just a brief moment in time. However, many people will deny this at all costs. Trust me, I know. Since we started doing the radio show in 1990, I have become somewhat of an honorary expert on wrestling. Over the years, I've been at countless social and family functions and there's always at least one person there to callously mock my endless devotion to such a "fake" sport, or to provide a smug snicker that they "outgrew" wrestling long ago. And yet, consistently, these are the same people who will wait until a quiet moment, when no one else is paying attention, to mention something inane, like they got to meet Koko B. Ware outside a Home Depot or that they dressed up like Demolition Axe for Halloween when they were in high school. If it just stopped there, it would probably be tolerable. But it never does. Instead, it's always followed up with: "And by the way, whatever happened to . . . ? I heard he died."

Death rumors have been around for ages. Kevin Sullivan recalled an instance where he was rumored dead in the early 1980s and Harley Race recalls learning he was dead as far back as the middle 1970s.

Dave Meltzer: There was a big rumor that Buddy Roberts was dead. This was long before the Internet and everyone in wrestling thought, in the dressing rooms, that he *was* dead. The rumors were ridiculous, because Buddy Roberts wasn't even missing bookings — he was still wrestling for Mid-South. I would go, "Look, the guy's on Mid-South TV every week!" But news traveled so slow. "No, no, no! He died." Hey, believe me, if he died, I would know.

Even wrestling newsletters and the Internet weren't enough to clear up the rumors that the Ultimate Warrior had died, sometime around 1992, and had been replaced by an imposter. This one really took on a life of it's own; in fact, we even bought it. And we were not alone.

Scott Hudson: When he came back, I don't know what had happened, I don't know if he had gotten off the gas or what his deal was, but when he came back he was wearing a singlet and they had to paint muscles on it. He looked just like Kerry Von Erich, and the rumor was he was wearing a singlet and they were painting muscles on him because it was a different guy, because the original Warrior's dead and this is a new guy stealing his gimmick or whatever. It was obviously the same guy and, well, he wasn't dead. But because of this drastic change in appearance, when Jim Hellwig came back everyone assumed it was a different person. So hey, if it's a different guy, the person must be dead. And then when WCW brought in Rick Wilson as the Renegade, that fed the rumor even more.

Bill Apter: Ultimate Warrior is still alive and he's the same guy.

PHANTOM

I think there were two Warriors, one that wrestled and one that's now touring the country as a Conservative Republican speaker. Neither of them makes any sense.

The two Warriors rumor became so widespread that even the Warrior himself became aware of it. In a 1997 Internet chat on Prodigy, Ultimate Warrior had this to say: "I've heard that rumor dozens of times, and the fact of the matter is you just don't react. Anytime you're in the public eye, people are going to make up rumors. You can't track down every rumor and the creator of every rumor. You just let it go."

Maybe the Ultimate Warrior was able to let it go, but wrestling fans have not. Just ask Viscera or Kevin Sullivan.

Viscera: I was receiving all kinds of phone calls from the Kat and Jerry Lawler and the office and they were asking me if I was okay. And I didn't know why. Then, when I got to work, I found out that somebody had put on the Internet that I had died in a car crash after dodging a cat and hitting a light pole.

Kevin Sullivan: There was a young wrestler called Ed "The Bull" Gantner. When Ed passed away his mother had a memorial service. And the only guys that went to the memorial service were me and Scott Hall. Somebody called my house and I wasn't home. And they kept on calling my house and I wasn't home. And then someone said, "Oh, he was at a memorial service." And the story became, I wasn't at a memorial service, there was a memorial service for me! And then it kept on going. How I died, the different ways I died. It's pretty amazing.

We could go on and on, but you get the point. No wrestler is immune: all it takes is one caring person to spread it around and you're forever affected. Sort of like herpes, just without the unsightly itching. And when the wrestling death rumor hits, old or young, big or small, wrestlers are always left scratching their heads. However, just like the Warrior, some wrestlers try and put it out of their mind and see the brighter side of things.

Jake Roberts: It's a good thing. You know why? It means that at least they're thinking about you. 'Cause there's a lot of guys out there who nobody remembers and they haven't been gone all that long.

Viscera: alive and well and looking for WWE divas

Viscera: It's kind of good to die before you die, you see how people feel about you. It really turned out to be a good deal, 'cause I found out that people do care a lot about me.

The common misconception amongst many wrestling fans is that these rumors are harmless. It's almost as if they believe the rumors are only spread within the confines of the locker room and wrestling's innermost circles. But that's the furthest thing from the truth.

SIR ADAM

It's always something like, "I don't even watch much anymore, but my cousin Pete does security at Nassau Coliseum and he overheard that the Undertaker was really buried alive and the guy replacing him is his next-door neighbor . . ."

PHANTOM

Get over the "non-wrestling fans drive you crazy" thing already.

SIR ADAM

Sorry, was I interrupting you whining about being afraid of Perry Saturn and the high school football team?

Even when we are able to confirm for a fellow fan that a wrestler believed to be dead is actually alive, the exchange always elicits a great deal of laughter. The stories become a part of wrestling folk-lore and travel all around the world. And more often than not, the rumor reaches a wrestler's friends and family — often before the wrestler learns of it himself.

Kamala: Right here in my hometown, they had it on the radio that I had passed away. My niece was listening to the radio, so she called me and my wife. We were out of town, and when we came in, we had a message on the machine. And then one of my sisters called me and she told me that she had heard it on the local radio station here too.

Matt Borne: There's been several rumors about me being dead over the years. One of the times was when I was in South Africa. My parents and all my relatives were getting all these phone calls — that I had died over there — and they contacted my wife. Luckily, my wife had just spoken to me . . .

Viscera: I'm glad my family didn't read the rumor before I could tell them that it was out there.

Traveling together and putting their lives in each others' hands every night, means the bond between wrestlers is almost familial.

Which is why they have such a tough time when they hear another death rumor involving one of their peers. Wrestlers fall prey to these rumors more frequently than you would imagine.

Justin Credible: I actually had one of my best friends in the business, Tony Devito, call my wife, and say, "Is Justin alright?"

Harley Race: I heard a rumor not long ago that Stan Hansen had passed on. I was actually reading something that said, "The late Stan Hansen." Well, I know Ted DiBiase lives right down there where Stan does, so I call him up. I said, surely this can't be true. He was too big in the business — basically in Japan — and I am still connected with a Japanese group. Had it been true, it would have been huge news. DiBiase said, "No, I don't think he is. I just talked to him."

Unfortunately, sometimes it's more than just a harmless rumor. Some "deaths" can't be disproven with a phone call. These rumors involve more than just an untruth, and often cause unbelievable problems in a wrestler's personal life. These days commercials warning against the danger of identity theft are everywhere. For wrestlers, it's not a new crisis.

Rumor-killer Harley Race

Jake Roberts: The weirdest thing was, one time, I got a call from Vince and he said, "What the hell have you done? They're going to kill you!" I'm like, "I just got home. What have I done? I don't know."

Some guy was impersonating me and married some Mafioso's daughter in Detroit, took her to the Cayman Islands and had been posing as me for, like, eight months. He married her, took her to the Cayman Islands, drugged her, beat the shit out of her, took all her jewelry, money, credit cards, and disappeared. I'm not through, it gets worse. This guy was following me around — and guess what I find out later? That son of a bitch was making more money than I was for personal appearances . . .

He got caught in Baltimore, because he called the hospital, said he was Jake "the Snake" and that he had a horrible neck injury. He needed a masseuse, he was in such pain. "Please, you've got to send someone over if you care anything about wrestling." And they sent a girl over there and he raped her. They finally got him with that and I had to carry papers with me for two years.

> Interesting, Jake, but your stories have always been a bit . . . unusual. As far as identity theft goes, it's not just "the Snake."

Matt Borne: I lost a passport once when I was living in Dallas, Texas. I was getting ready to go to South Africa and I carried this bag which had my passport in there, a little bit of cash and all my ID. And I left it on top of a phone booth about three blocks from the Sportatorium in Dallas. Several years passed and when '97 came along, somebody in Salt Lake City OD'd. He had my social, my name, everything. He had my identity. Actually, I had an outstanding bench warrant for failure to appear for some stupid thing like public drunkenness or something like that. So they ran a check, this guy OD's in Salt Lake City and they have him in a hospital and so they run a check on him and they see there's this outstanding warrant from Pennsylvania. So they contact the borough where the warrant was from and they said, "Well, this Matt Osborne just OD'd, and when we get him back around, do you want him?" Later, they called back and said, "He died." So whoever had my identity died.

> We witnessed perhaps the strangest impersonation of all time, first-hand. In July 2001, a comedy club in New York City was promoting that wrestling's own Iron Sheik would be doing a stand-up set. That's right, the Iron Sheik. Not Bobby Heenan, not Jerry Lawler — the Iron Sheik. If you've ever had the "pleasure"

of listening to the Iron Sheik speak, you know: this was a can't-miss event.

SIR ADAM

I remember waking up one morning and reading on a wrestling website that the Iron Sheik was going to be doing stand-up comedy at Caroline's in New York City. Not more than thirty seconds later Phantom calls me in a state of shock, asking if this could possibly be true. I mean, we've probably had Sheik on our show ten times over the years, and spoken with him off the air on countless other occasions, but in all that time all he ever talked about was how he beat Hogan in Madison Square Garden and that he was an Olympic champion. That was the joke. That he had no clue what was going on around him. So Sheik made me laugh a lot over the years, but I don't think he ever knew it, or that it was anything intentional. There was no way we were missing this.

PHANTOM

We went to the club, and the guy on stage looked like the Sheik's identical twin. Even Sir Adam did a double take. The tip off was that when he spoke, we could actually understand him.

SIR ADAM

We left the show and I called my wife and had her pull up our contact list on my computer. We called the Iron Sheik while we were standing outside the club and, as we suspected, he was at home in Georgia. We went back inside and tried to confront the imposter, but everyone in the club thought we were just being dicks. We were thrown out.

PHANTOM

The next day, I couldn't believe that no one in the comedy club believed us, so I fired off a heated e-mail to 1wrestling.com. Little

The real Elephant Boy and the real Iron Sheik with our heros

did I know that the story was picked up by national radio talk show hosts Opie and Anthony. They not only read my e-mail on the air, but they spoke extensively on the subject and mentioned *Get in the Ring Radio*. A co-worker was listening and was shocked that O & A were mentioning my show. He called me and as soon as he got the words out I was dialing up WNEW studios in New York. I got on air and talked with the guys about the fake Sheik and the possibility that Stephanie McMahon had breast implants — really heady stuff. It was a highlight in my miserable radio career, and I have Fake Comedian Iron Sheik Guy to thank. Thanks Fake Comedian Iron Sheik Guy.

We can understand why someone would start a rumor that Fake Comedian Iron Sheik Guy had expired, but why are wrestling fans so eager to put their heroes in their graves? The best answer seems to come from resident GIR Psychologist Edward R. Friedrich, long time listeners will remember him fondly as "Club" Ed.

"Club" Ed, Ph.D.: While professional wrestling is largely based on a combination of athleticism and storytelling, it is undeniable that there are strong elements of aggression and violence contained within each and every match. It is indisputable that part of wrestling's appeal lies in its sheer brutality. Think about it. In your ordinary day-to-day life you can argue with someone you don't like, and maybe even get away with throwing a punch. But if you piledrive them on cement and then hit them over the head with a steel chain, don't expect to ever eat a meal off of anything other than a metal plate slid through a small opening in a door. In wrestling, you can live out every sick and twisted fantasy you ever had. Only in wrestling can you watch the guy who hit on your woman being beaten senseless with a two by four without suffering any consequences. Only in wrestling can you see the guy who made fun of your ethnicity get suplexed off a ladder and through a table. Of course wrestling fans are of a different breed than hardcore figure skating fans. Wrestling fans possess something darker than the members of the Brian Boitano fan club. And with this comes the tendency to believe that the reason Kevin Sullivan is no longer wrestling on your TV set each week is not because he wants to spend time with his family, travel, or is simply tired of the wear and tear on his body, but rather because he has suffered a horrible death.

Kevin Sullivan: Once you're off TV, the character dies. They're looking for something, a reason you're not on TV. Rumors just start . . .

Scott Hudson: In other sports, when someone retires, they're not necessarily gone from the spotlight. If they're playing major league ball and they retire or get waived and don't get picked up, you'll still see them on the air, commentating or whatever. In wrestling it's all or nothing.

Bill Apter: Wrestling fans have always been fast to think someone's dead if they don't see him.

> One line of thinking we encountered is that the rumors are actually started by other grapplers. Wrestlers are well-known for

pulling pranks or ribs. Often, the most legendary pranks are those where the payoff takes place outside of the locker room.

Ron Garvin: I remember Terry Garvin used to do it to a lot of people. He would call a newspaper somewhere and he'd say so and so was dead. I remember one time, he called a newspaper and he said that Tony Santos, a promoter in Boston, had passed away. You know, because Tony Santos had played a rib on him. So he was getting back at him.

Bobby Heenan: Remember when we were kids in high school? She put out, she didn't. She'll let you feel her up, she won't. You know what wrestling is? Wrestling is high school, but we got money.

Another prevalent theory is that the hard lifestyle many wrestlers lead is to blame. We've all seen the exposés and heard the stories about wrestlers taking pain pills, indulging in recreational "medication" and just plain hitting the town. Well, when you read enough and you hear enough, it makes some people believe the worst.

Reno: I think it has a lot to do with wrestlers, because we're dropping like flies. Unfortunately, we all party like rock stars — and we're not. Your body can only take so much and . . . Actually, wrestlers do a whole lot more stupid shit than rock stars.

Justin Credible: I was still with WWE. I just wasn't on television and wasn't being used. And I was probably partying harder than I should have, so I think somewhere, somehow the rumor started that I died, which was obviously not true.

Matt Borne: I think it's the whole aura . . . A friend of mine was telling me that he saw a list on some news broadcast of all of the occupations that are real hazardous to your health and pro wrestler was at the top.

Scott Hudson: People that are still fans now, who became fans with Hulk Hogan in '85, they're seeing the people they grew up with die because they're screwing around with pills, or in car wrecks or whatever. Death is really catching up to wrestling . . . People that I grew up watching are dying because of old age, and the people that the twenty and twenty-five year olds grew up watching are dying because of pills and whatever . . .

PHANTOM

Damn you! Why are you so smart, Scott Hudson?

Many wrestlers offer valid explanations, but here's the one we liked the best . . . (After all, is there anyone in wrestling more profound than the "Living Legend"?)

Larry Zbyszko: I don't know if it's wrestling fans, it's probably human nature. We all get up in the morning and deny the fact that we're going to die. Shit, you might as well just stay home and say, "Why should I do anything? I'm gonna be dead in 20 years." If I die they'll give me a three-bell ceremony for ten seconds and then talk about the upcoming Pay-per-view. If you turn on the news and they go, "Oh my God, Bob Hope died," it's almost as if death is reminding you it's there. It's a little personal confrontation everyone has with their own death when they hear someone famous or someone well-known has died.

So, will the rumors ever stop? Unfortunately, with so much information on the Internet, it doesn't seem likely. At the same time, the Internet should help combat the problem.

Wade Keller: I think that, at this point, with the Internet being so accessible, there's a greater majority of people who say, "You know what, I'm just going to look around for a while before asking a dumb question." It doesn't take too long to have a lot of questions answered.

Dave Meltzer: Ten years ago rumors spread pretty quick, and obviously, with the Internet they spread much quicker. I remember there were death rumors then, but now there's more of them and they get around quicker. And they probably get disproven quicker, too. A Paul Orndorff death rumor today would be disproven within a day — not six months.

And so, by a unanimous two to nothing margin, we've decided that the all-time greatest wrestling death rumor is whether or not Paul Orndorff actually expired in the early '90s. In fact, by another unanimous vote, it's also been voted the most annoying question in *Get in the Ring* history. Now, let's get to it . . . Well, we're happy to report that he's fine and . . . crazy. Excuse us, he's "bipolar." You see, Paul came on our radio show in June of 2003 and made the startling revelation that he was then recently diagnosed with bipolar disorder. But the question remains after all these years.

Paul, have you heard the rumors?

The *biggest death rumor of the '90s*

Paul "Mr. Wonderful" Orndorff: Yeah I have, they must be getting me mixed up with some of these guys who've been dying lately. I don't know the meaning behind it . . .

Paul believes the rumors started when he left wrestling and opened a bowling alley. Mostly, he heard about them from friends. He attributes a lot of it to the level of popularity he reached during his heyday, and how fans and other wrestlers still talk about him today. However, what's more amazing is that the rumors don't phase him.

Paul "Mr. Wonderful" Orndorff: I do nothing; it does nothing to me. I have nothing to say: good, bad, or in the middle. I just don't know what they think they're doing it for . . .

Everyone else we spoke with was concerned. Why not Paul?

Paul "Mr. Wonderful" Orndorff: To be quite honest with you, I've found out lately that I'm nuts, and back then I didn't even know I was damn nuts, so people think that this was a put on. No man, that's the way I am — ask my family. I wasn't on no medicine and I could use my rage in the ring. Hulk said he never knew what I'd be like each night. That's a shoot man, I'm telling you as I look back, my poor wife, my family . . .

At least he's still alive!

Chapter 9

Are Referees Blind?

Jake Roberts: They can help you, or they can bury you. Wrestling is the only dance for three. Someone misses a step, then you're gone.

At first glance, you might think that the skills required to become a professional wrestling referee are on par with those of a zookeeper or rodeo clown, but the truth is, a referee is far more important to a good match than most people think. In fact, we interviewed a number of referees for this book, and believe it or not, they were intelligent, well-spoken individuals. The idea that they're a step slower than you? Well, it's something that actually helps create wrestling magic.

The year is 1986 and Tito Santana is defending the Intercontinental title against Randy "Macho Man" Savage in the famed Boston Garden. Savage reaches into his trunks, pulls out a foreign object — which the late Gorilla Monsoon describes only as a piece of "cold rolled steel" — and knocks Tito senseless.

The entire arena saw it, even the people up in the cheap seats. Surely, the referee noticed this flagrant attempt to circumvent the rules, right? Nope. The ref counted to three, Savage was the new champion and fans could only yell: "Are you kidding me? What, are you blind, ref?"

A.J. Styles: Referees, they gotta let some stuff fly, they can't just call everything. Just like in the NBA. I'm sure they see a little hand slapping here and there, but they're not gonna call it, because if they called every foul it would be boring, no one would want to watch it. It would be just a bunch of foul shots, and Shaq would be losing the game for everyone.

Larry Zbyszko: They have to be there at the right time, for the right count, to make sure there's suspense. A referee's timing is just as important as a wrestler's timing. So a bad referee, or an inexperienced referee, can really mess up the whole finish. Referees can be *very* blind — but then, sometimes that's good.

Referee Daryl Lankford: Basically, what it comes down to is that we have to turn a blind eye every now and then . . .

> Think about the main event of WrestleMania I. On one side of the ring stood the legendary "Mr. Wonderful" Paul Orndorff and everyone's most hated villain, "Rowdy" Roddy Piper. And on the other side, the incomparable Hulk Hogan and Hollywood's own Mr. T. Arguably, this was the biggest match in the history of the sport. Let's be honest, the grandeur and mystique of WrestleMania I changed the industry forever. It took wrestling out of the dark ages and set the stage for the sports entertainment spectacular it is today. So, whether you were there in person, saw it on closed circuit TV, or even if you just watched it on video, odds are you still remember that match. The date: March 31, 1985. The place: Madison Square Garden. A sold out crowd was crazy with anticipation. After thirteen minutes of action, the heroes defeated the team of Orndorff and Piper after Cowboy Bob Orton's attempt to interfere on behalf of the treacherous duo backfired. So who was the referee that counted to three that night?
>
> You don't know, do you?
>
> Don't worry, let's try again.
>
> Seventeen years later: March 17, 2002. The Skydome in Toronto, Canada is the site. Hulk Hogan makes his triumphant return to the main event of WrestleMania X-8. This time he battles the

Rock, in a match that pits the greatest from the past against the Great One from the present. If you're reading this book, you saw it. Approximately 68,200 people watched live, and the event registered one of the largest Pay-per-view audiences in history, with approximately 840,000 buys. So, who was the referee for this colossal encounter? It wasn't Pat Patterson, who refereed the WrestleMania I main event. The answer is: Mike Chioda. And again, you didn't know. Or at least you shouldn't have.

Referee Charles Robinson: You know, the guys don't like for us to be seen at all. If you don't notice the referee that means he is doing a pretty good job. That is, unless he's just standing there in the corner and not moving at all.

Sir Adam making sure WWE ref Charles Robinson stays honest

Jimmy Valiant: A good referee? You don't know he's there because he's doing his job, we're doing our jobs. Everything blends in. Of course, if he's in your way . . . yeah, he can make or break it.

Larry Zbyszko: You wouldn't even remember who the referee was unless something special was going on . . . but the referee is very important.

> We don't remember — because we aren't supposed to! Seems easy enough, but the more we talked to people in the business, the more we realized that a good referee does more than just stay out of the way and make the three count. It's actually a very difficult job — one that requires great timing, quick thinking and skill.

Referee Daryl Lankford: Sometimes you have to be in the right spot at the right time; you have to kind of give them a hand every now and then. There's a lot more involved than just counting three.

Referee Rudy Charles: You're telling a story and you want the crowd to believe it.

Referee Jamie Tucker: It's hard to keep order while we're in there. Some people don't understand that. It's a hard job: to stand there and stay in between two big guys, sometimes four, sometimes six, even eight . . . And it gets rough, and puts us in compromising positions . . .

> All the legendary matches in professional wrestling history share one common characteristic: they told a captivating story. And if you compare wrestling matches to movies, try to think of the referee as the guy up for the best supporting actor Oscar.

Referee Rudy Charles: I think false finishes and stuff like that can really add to a match. There's all sorts of little things that go on that people don't realize — like when you get messages from the back.

> While a baseball umpire or a basketball official are supposed to view the game objectively, the wrestling referee is a part of the

show. In fact, they are so much a part of the performance that almost all of the wrestlers we spoke with agreed that a prerequisite to putting on a great match is having a referee who is performing at the top of his game.

Harley Race: A good referee can damn sure help make a match. The guys in the ring have to respect his ability. You know, it's a two way street.

A.J. Styles: Refs are also used to relay messages between wrestlers. If I say, "Hey, tell him to do this to me," the ref will go check on him and say this to the other wrestler. And then we'll get up and we'll keep going without talking to each other. I'd say they play a huge part, when it comes to the wrestling. You can be confident that you're gonna have a good match when you have a good ref.

Jake Roberts: If the ref is paying proper attention, he makes it look interesting. He is interested; he reacts to what you're doing. If you are selling as a babyface and it's a terrific shot, if he reacts, then it's a terrific shot. The fans look at everybody in the ring, and everybody's reaction is what they buy.

So while the majority of fans may discount their roles, referees can sleep easy, knowing that their efforts are not overlooked by the wrestlers themselves. It is this respect that has lead many wrestlers to request, and actually fight for certain referees to officiate their matches.

Buff Bagwell: There's a lot of finishes that require a good bit of talent on the part of a referee. So that's why certain refs get certain matches.

A.J. Styles: If you're gonna bump one, you want to get the one who knows how to take that bump and make it look good.

Okay, okay. We're sorry referees. We apologize for calling you blind and stupid and for throwing peanuts at you all these years. You're important. And it seems, from our research, the best example of what makes a good referee is embodied in the work of Earl Hebner. Hebner has been a referee for over twenty years and has been in the middle of the action for such legendary confrontations as Hulk Hogan versus Andre the Giant and "Stone Cold" Steve Austin versus the Rock. So, what makes Earl so special?

Referee Charles Robinson: You know I've learned a lot from Earl, just in the past two and a half years I've worked with him. He's a leader.

Harley Race: Earl Hebner is a hell of a referee. He knows what to do himself in the ring and he does not get in your way.

Referee Rudy Charles: He has a good knowledge of wrestling. He's at the right position at the right time. He's been doing it for I don't know how many years, but he always seems to know exactly where he's at in the ring.

Jake Roberts: A good heel respects authority, he backs off. "Sir, I'm sorry." When the referee turns his back, he goes around him: that's how a heel gets heat. Not nine guys jumping one, that's not heat, that's disgust. So a good referee is very, very important, and Earl is one of the best.

Any good referee knows they must be physical in the ring, that their gestures help fans comprehend certain aspects of a match. This includes indicating a rule violation or close counts. However, one characteristic that sets the good referees apart is their ability to communicate effectively. This aspect of a referee's job is crucial, both to selling the story being presented to the fans, and to working with the participants. Earl is amongst the best in this regard.

Referee Daryl Lankford: You want to make sure the wrestlers hear you, because if you're in the middle of something and their mind's somewhere else or they've got an injury nagging them, they may not know where the count's going or what they're doing. Earl is a guy you can hear all the time.

Since Earl is apparently very verbal in the ring, we called him to get his take on what makes him special. Apparently, he's not too verbal at home — he never called us back. But this comes as no surprise, he probably remembers the Sid Vicious incident.

SIR ADAM

At one point we actually had a good working relationship with WWE. They would regularly purchase advertising time on our show and supply us with tickets and guests. It was great.

PHANTOM

Yeah until Sir Adam said he hated Triple H.

SIR ADAM

You know, that could have been it. Anyway, sometime around 1997, Sid Vicious was one of the top stars in the company and was making an autograph appearance in Brooklyn, NY, about an hour away from where we lived. We had Sid on the show before and were sure he would be happy to speak with us. We called the office and arranged to get a few minutes with Sid right before the signing. However, one of the Hebners (we were told it was Earl, but they're twins, so who knows for sure), told us we would have to wait until it was over. So we waited outside the building for two hours and when Sid left the building that damn Hebner pushed our tape recorder away and told Sid to get in the limo so they could leave.

PHANTOM

All we got was a promo that said, "This is Psycho Sid, and I wanna, I wanna *Get in the Ring.*" Good promo, but not worth two hours.

David Flair and ref Charles Robinson

David Flair: I've never been in a match with Earl Hebner, but he and his brother are the best.

While we may prefer Mary Kate and Ashley Olsen when it comes to twins (and we're positive Bret Hart is no fan of anyone named Hebner, but more on that fateful night in Montreal later), according to David Flair, his father Ric has named Dave and Earl Hebner, Charles Robinson, Nick Patrick and especially Tommy Young as his favorite referees to work with. Now, let's talk about Tommy Young. He was a referee for approximately fifteen years, spending most of his career in the Mid-Atlantic territory. He is widely regarded as one of the greatest of all time and has presided over such classic matches as Ric Flair versus Ricky Steamboat, Ric Flair versus Terry Funk and Magnum T.A. versus Nikita Koloff.

Jimmy Valiant: I'll tell you the truth, brother. Tommy Young is probably one of the greatest referees there is.

Referee Jamie Tucker: Growing up, I would always look at the referee's work. Obviously, that's why I'm doing this now. Tommy Young is my favorite to watch.

We're happy to report that Tommy is also a very nice guy — and he was more than happy to talk to us for this book.

PHANTOM

Actually, he wouldn't shut up.

SIR ADAM

In fact, if you are in North Carolina, anywhere in North Carolina, and you listen very closely, you can still hear him talking.

In Tommy's words, here is what typified the in-ring style that earned him his stellar reputation . . .

Referee Tommy Young: I tell all referees that it is our job to make the wrestler's job easier. And I will tell the wrestlers in the dressing room — or I did when I was active — I'll work with you in any way I can, but please don't make a fool out of me. Don't do things right in front of me. Because people are going to see it and I'll have to respond to it. But if you work at trying to hide something, and I feel it's done right, because I'm always trying to feel the people, I'll let you do it all night. The problem is you don't want to disgust the crowd, because if you do, they're probably not coming back. Or they're going to have such a bitter taste in their mouths that they're not going to want to come back.

Over the course of his career, Young presided over many of The Nature Boy's most legendary championship matches. Tommy told us about putting his own stamp on a classic Ric Flair spot.

Referee Tommy Young: He likes to work along the ropes. We would do a move where he'd grab a guy in an armlock and stand close to the ropes. I would slide in there, underneath, asking the guy if he wants to give up. And while I'm doing that Flair is grabbing the top rope, right over my head, for leverage. Soon, people are screaming — I'll always look at the people first — that would telegraph it to the wrestler, that I'm getting ready to look. So, when I look at the people, that's kind of his cue to quit doing it because they're gonna point and then I'm gonna look. The smart wrestler lets go, doesn't hold the rope anymore. There's nobody touching it. Maybe it's vibrating a little bit. "Hey, you touching that rope?" I ask. "No I'm not touching it," he goes. "Don't listen to those idiots."

> Tommy's approach was relatively simple, but very effective. He exhibited a great deal of respect for the fans and recognized that there is a delicate relationship between them and the sport. He did his best to preserve what was best for the organization he worked for, even if it meant some of the wrestlers had to work harder in the ring. In doing so, he irritated some guys along the way. The great ones, however, appreciated his efforts.

Bobby Eaton: Tommy made it look like he was really trying to get in there if you pulled someone's hair in front of him, which I've been guilty of. He makes you sneaky. That helped you out. If you can do it in front of a ref, then there's no reason to cheat.

Referee Tommy Young: With the 1-2-3 count for a pinfall, I'd say, "Guys, if your shoulders are down, I'm gonna have to count you out, so for God's sake, get them up." And I did count out some wrestlers during my career who were just lazy and figured I'd protect them. No! The office didn't want me to protect them. They said, if they're laying on their lazy asses, you count them out.

Referee Charles Robinson: Fact of the matter is, if someone doesn't kick out, we should count them out.

> Many people have asked us over the years, can a bad referee ruin a match between two good wrestlers? The answer is simple: an ineffective or poorly trained referee can absolutely ruin what was potentially a good match. It's like this: if the '80s band Winger had a drummer who couldn't keep a beat, it wouldn't matter how much Kip Winger rocked, they would still sound awful . . .

Referee Jamie Tucker: A bad ref can ruin a match. You might as well go ahead and put a broomstick in there . . .

> A referee can throw off an intricately laid out match by not knowing the finish. The wrestlers are down on the mat, the ref hits the mat, *one, two* . . . And then it's supposed to be *three*. But the ref isn't sure, so he barely taps the canvas. This screws up everything, leaving fans and wrestlers alike wondering if the match is actually over.

A.J. Styles: I'll give you another example. I was in a six-man not too long ago. The ref didn't stop me from coming into the ring illegally. And if the ref doesn't pull me back when I'm not supposed to be in there, I'm gonna go after a guy. So it won't look like a goof, I gotta go in there and start hitting him.

Jake Roberts: You try to get a quick pin on a guy or a sunset flip on a guy and he takes ten seconds to get down there? If they're not concerned about the violence that's going on, the cheating, the good, the bad, the whatever — if they let the heel get away with too much — then they look like an idiot. Let me ask you a question. If there is a sniper shooting kids at a school ground, and there is a policeman standing next to him with a gun, but he's not doing anything, where's the heat? On the policeman, right? A bad referee gets the heat, not the heel.

> Okay, we've seen how a referee affects a match as an authority fig-ure, but referees are also frequently required to get involved physically. It's not just wrestlers who get thrown around the ring. Even though their size usually pales in comparison to the com-batants, referees often must endure the same punishment. In fact, most referees go all out when they take bumps, encouraging wrestlers not to hold anything back.

Referee Daryl Lankford: For myself, I've always told the wrestlers to go full force, don't hold anything back. The way I look at it, even the referees, if you can't take a bump every now and then, and occasionally it gets a little harder than you would like, but if you can't take one every now and then, you probably don't belong in the business.

Referee Tommy Young: Most WWE referees are good. I saw a match where the Big Show went to kick somebody and the guy ducked and he kicked the referee and knocked the referee right out of the ring. I tell you, I don't think I could have taken a bump that good. That bump was phenomenal.

> Of course, becoming physically involved in the action means there are bound to be a number of injuries.

Referee Charles Robinson: On the independent circuit before I got on with WCW, I had my elbow kicked out of its socket. Needless to say, I did not stay in the ring and continue the match. I rolled out and left. Left the guys just standing in the ring. Probably not the best thing to do, but that's what I did. I earned my ten dollars that night.

Referee Rudy Charles: If I may, one of the worst injuries I ever had was from a Dusty Rhodes' bionic elbow . . .

Referee Jamie Tucker: I've had my knee pop out of place. I also broke my finger during a match. Nothing to keep me from doing it, but the pain's there . . .

PHANTOM

> A lot of people don't realize the dangers we're subjected to. One time Sir Adam "accidentally" tangled my headphones and I started choking.

SIR ADAM

> Thank God Tom, our seventy year old engineer, was there to give you mouth-to-mouth.

PHANTOM

You never get tired of telling that story, do you?

There are many misconceptions about a referee's job, but what the find perhaps most frustrating are preconceived notions about their physical conditioning. It's not easy, keeping up with the guys in the ring. It takes training and endurance.

Referee Daryl Lankford: On an average show, if there's ten matches, we'll have two referees. We're up and down, we're all around. We have to be moving all the time. Sometimes the fans don't realize, we go through a lot.

Referee Charles Robinson: One thing seems to have changed in the business. If you look at old tapes, most of your referees were old, fat guys. Nowadays, the referees, we work out every day, we train. That's important. We've really changed the face of the job, we're younger and a little bit better looking. You have to be in shape, with the way that guys move around the ring now. It's not old school, where you grab a hold for five to ten minutes. A sixty minute match, back then . . . well, you were in a rest hold for forty minutes. With the cruiserweights . . . these guys are going ten to twelve minutes, but they're going full blast the whole time.

Unfortunately, in the ring, things don't always go as planned. The best wrestlers often improvise, and many times the finish of a match will be altered at the last minute in response to the crowd reaction.

Referee Charles Robinson: It happened to me with Ric Flair and Diamond Dallas Page. They did the diamond cutter and that wasn't supposed to be the finish, but they had changed it without telling me and I didn't count Flair out.

Dealing with a missed finish is one thing, but when someone is injured in the ring — that's when a referee is really called to action. In those instances, referees play a vital role, both with the wrestlers involved and with people in the back. The referee can make a crucial difference: preventing potentially career-ending, even life-threatening injuries from becoming worse. The word used to communicate such a serious injury is "kayfabe."

Referee Daryl Lankford: That's the code word most referees use. At that point, if it's serious enough you just stop and call the match. You definitely have to communicate and if you don't get the word out fast enough you could aggravate an injury in a heartbeat. Any time somebody's down and hurt and you know it, and it's not part of the planned match, you definitely got to tell the other workers that its kayfabed. You're looking out for each other.

Referee Charles Robinson: Probably the worst injury that I've been

Tommy Young giving GIR the scoop on refs

in the ring with was Fit Finlay and the Nasty Boys — when Fit had the back of his leg ripped off. You could tell he wasn't faking because his calf was lying off in the middle of the ring. You know, in situations like that, you just end the match, just stop the match. Something like that, where someone's just not moving, you try and communicate with the guy and hopefully he'll respond to let you know if he's okay or not. They ask all the time after a big move if a guy is okay and we'll give the signal if they're fine. Of course, we'll give the big cross if they're not.

Referee Rudy Charles: I was doing a hardcore match one time back in my younger days and a guy's arm got caught in the barbed wire, like three seconds into the match, and I had to stop the match because he couldn't get out of it.

Referee Tommy Young: I remember one time we were in Shelby, North Carolina and Don Kernodle ripped his whole elbow open on the hook that hooked the turnbuckle to the ring. It was a horrible injury, a lot of blood.

Referee Rudy Charles: New Jack went off the top of the balcony — he landed pretty hard and they had to call an ambulance for him, which was a little scary. I know he's done a lot of crazy things over the years, but still I hate to see someone get hurt like that. And the ambulance came and checked on him and they wanted to take him to the hospital. But they didn't, he wouldn't let them.

New Jack (from an 11/04 *GIR Radio* Interview): Because I don't give a fuck . . .

> Of course, any chapter on refereeing would be incomplete without addressing that controversial night in November, 1997, and what is commonly referred to as the "Montreal Screwjob." At the time, Bret Hart was the WWF champion, but he was also just about to leave the federation for WCW. Understandably, Vince McMahon did not want to risk Bret showing up on WCW television with the WWF World Title belt. So, Hart was asked to drop the strap to Shawn Michaels on the Survivor Series Pay-per-view.

Throughout the years, however, Hart and Michaels had a real, heated, and well-documented rivalry. Because of this, Hart invoked the creative control clause in his contract, and refused the request. Faced with a difficult dilemma, Vince McMahon made the decision: Hart was going to drop the belt in Montreal, whether he wanted to or not.

The match proceeded, and after much intense brawling, Michaels finally placed Hart in his own finishing move, the Sharpshooter. Almost instantly, McMahon, who had strutted down to the ring, began screaming: "Ring the fucking bell!" The ref signaled for the bell and ducked out of the ring. The only problem? Hart never submitted. He was sticking to what he thought was the script. Hart had been told that the match would end with a disqualification — and that he could forfeit the title on an upcoming *Raw*. After seeing his title awarded to Michaels, Hart realized he'd been duped. He proceeded to spit the most disgusting "loogee" ever recorded on film right at Vince's head. Michaels, looking confused, left with the belt and without any of the typical post-match fanfare that accompanies a world title change. HBK's level of involvement became the topic of much debate in the years following the incident, and he has only recently admitted to knowing the game plan all along. Despite proceeding to punch out his boss in the dressing room, and having his name attached to the most interesting incident in wrestling folklore, some argue Hart has never gotten over the incident.

The Montreal Screwjob illustrates that a referee can, at times, play the *biggest* part in a match. In this case, it was Earl Hebner's job to make the finish look as legitimate as possible — even without the cooperation of one of the participants. The way the event unfolded proves just how much power a referee holds.

Prior to the Survivor Series, a suspicious Hart had asked Hebner, his long-time friend, whether anyone was planning to screw around with the finish. Essentially, Hebner replied that the match would go on as planned. Bret Hart has stated publicly that he was deeply hurt by Hebner's involvement in the incident. So did Earl make the right decision, not telling Bret what was going

Hebner, Bret and Owen Hart

to happen? We asked our panel of referees what they would have done if they found themselves in the same situation.

Referee Charles Robinson: Exact same thing, period. Vince McMahon is the boss. What he says to do, you do. I'm sorry, that's the way it is. He is the boss and you do what he says. He's paying the bills. Bret Hart is not paying the bills. Shawn Michaels wasn't paying the bills. Those guys can't fire me, Vince McMahon can. I do what Vince says.

Referee Daryl Lankford: Whew, that's probably one of the toughest things . . . because from a personal standpoint I have a lot of respect for Bret Hart, for what he's done for the business and what he's meant to the business. Thinking about that, and if I was in that situation . . . Obviously, it's my main source of income, [if] I'm on the road working for the biggest company there is, and I know there's a very good chance that if I don't do it that I probably don't have a job, or my job's going to be made a living hell . . . It really makes you think. I guess what it comes down to is, it's your job. And where does your loyalty lie? I probably would have to say I would go with the boss, and hope that, in the end, if I was pretty close with a wrestler . . . they would understand. That's probably one of the toughest situations a referee could be in.

Referee Tommy Young: I would have had to listen to Vince. I mean, the question is, who do you want heat with, Bret Hart or Vince McMahon? Who's signing your check? That answers that.

Referee Rudy Charles: I can definitely sympathize with Brett Hart . . . but at the same time I sympathize with Hebner, because if he didn't do it, that's his job. And the thing is, if he didn't do it, they would have found somebody that would . . .

Referee Jamie Tucker: Earl was put in a compromising position . . . Nobody knows the whole situation . . . If my job was on the line, I'd probably lean towards [doing the same thing] — you've got to be a company guy.

The referees have been heard. But what about Hart's side of the story?

Bret Hart (from a 12/97 *GIR Radio* Interview): I pulled Earl aside, days before, in Detroit, Michigan. He broke into tears, pretty much, 'cause I think it was a very emotional time. And to be honest, I don't think Earl lied to me that night. He broke down and told me that he swore on his children that he would never do anything, that they could never talk him into screwing me out of the title . . . He would quit his job first; he would never do it; he would never fall for it. He basically gave me every kind of assurance that it would never, ever, ever, ever happen. And I believed him. The next night, when he was getting ready to walk from the dressing room — I'm understanding this from second or third parties now, I've never talked to him or anybody else in the office since that black day — he was apparently told . . . that they were going to screw me out of the belt. And the problem I have with that is that he said that he would quit. And he said he would not allow it to happen. And he went in there and did it, without even blinking an eye.

I was warned by everyone, for days, to be very careful. And I was very, very careful. I thought that they would have to have a referee partake in this thing. If someone asked me — and that's why I fell victim to it so easily — if someone would have asked me whether Earl Hebner would burn me, I'd say, "There's no way Earl Hebner would ever play a part in anything like this." And you know, I had people suggest that he had a family and, you know, his job was on the line — and I understand all that. But at the same time, he assured me that job or no job — hell, he swore on his own child — that I wouldn't need to worry about it. And that's the problem I have: he should have told me in Detroit, "If they put a gun to my head, I got to do what they tell me." In which case, I would have been very careful about holds, or when [Michaels was] covering me for a pinfall. They wouldn't have got past two.

We've been thinking about this situation for years, and we still don't know what we would have done. What it does make us realize is that referees are under-appreciated — skilled performers who are forced to make difficult, high-pressure decisions and then get the crap kicked out of them on a regular basis.

So, why become a referee in the first place?

Referee Charles Robinson: Why? Big fan of Ric Flair. Ever since, probably, '74 or '75. It's always been a dream to work with him, and that's why I got into the business.

Referee Rudy Charles: I always wanted to be a referee. I started refereeing soccer in the eighth grade and I've always enjoyed refereeing. I guess it would be fun, wrestlers get all the glory, but everybody plays a part and I think if I were ever to be a wrestler, I guarantee I wouldn't be that good. I'm a better referee than I could ever be a wrestler and I think that's how I can contribute.

Referee Jamie Tucker: Growing up, I was a big wrestling fan. Always thought I wanted to become a wrestler. But I've come to realize I wasn't athletically gifted like a lot of the guys. Wasn't that big either. And when I was growing up, you had to be a big guy to be in this business. It wasn't like it is now, with the cruiserweights and so on.

How I broke in the business is: I was fifteen years of age and I was actually just thrown in the ring at a pro wrestling show. I just knew a bunch of the guys, and the promoter needed a referee. I was thrown in there and since day one I've been hooked.

Referee Charles Robinson: I like to have rules to enforce. In fact, now, when I do a tables match or hardcore match or something like that, it's no fun. You stand in there and you try to look like you're involved, and you're not. You're there to make a three count, or whatever . . . ring the bell when the table breaks.

Referee Jamie Tucker: The average person probably doesn't give the referees their due. They think anybody could do the job. But if they were ever put in our position, in our shoes, I wouldn't think it would come out the same. Not everybody can do the job.

Next time you're watching a match and a referee misses a ball shot, chair shot, hair pull, eye gouge or, even worse, gets "knocked into the middle of next week," remember: he isn't blind or incompetent; he's just doing his job. In fact, he might actually get a raise . . .

Chapter 10

Is Hulk Hogan the Best Friend a Wrestler Can Have?

Alan Funk: I wish *I* was his best friend.

Chances are even your grandmother knows who Hulk Hogan is. Without a doubt, whether you are in Japan, England, India or Cleveland, he's still one of the most recognizable athletes in the world. So it's no surprise that in the thirteen year history of *Get in the Ring Radio*, Hogan's name comes up at some point during almost every single interview. Everyone has a Hulk Hogan story, and he can make even long-time wrestlers revert back into simple fans.

Chris Kanyon: I was there in '84 when Hogan won the belt . . .

Of course, when you reach Hogan's level of success, you are also open to a certain amount of criticism. And the Hulkster has had more than his share.

Jake Roberts: I was going to offer him a trip to my wrestling school . . .

Sean Waltman: Hulk was never considered Ric Flair/Ricky Steamboat type shit. But guess what? He made the people scream.

Bam Bam Bigelow (From a 3/02 *GIR Radio* Interview): God bless him, he did a lot for this business. His popularity helped everybody get to where they are today. But at the same time, you can drag it down. I mean, when you lose it in the ring you should find something different to do. Look at what Jesse Ventura did with announcing. Now he's a former governor. Maybe Hogan should try it.

Jimmy Hart modeling the world's worst suit

PHANTOM

When we started the show, we were still in high school. The biggest thrill we had in those days was getting Terry Funk to unleash his hatred for Hulk Hogan.

SIR ADAM

We had no idea that when we asked Terry, "What do you think about Hulk Hogan?" we'd get the greatest trash talking in GIR history. Unfortunately, being stupid kids, we never taped the show.

PHANTOM

Because Sir Adam never taped the diatribe, we invited Funk back five years later to try to recreate the sheer hatred and contempt.

(From an 8/96 *GIR Radio* Interview)

Sir Adam: What are your feelings towards Hulk Hogan?

Terry Funk: Right now, as I've reached this stage in my life, it certainly isn't admiration . . . but I don't have a hatred towards anybody anymore. And I don't know if it's because I've gotten older or I've reached an age when I'm beginning to mellow.

Phantom: Terry, you're mellowing? No way!

Terry Funk: I really wonder. I see some things that I would have done differently . . . I am not a fan of Hogan's, nor do I adore his work ethic in the ring.

PHANTOM

Unfortunately, Funk had turned a corner in his life, refusing to unleash like he had five years earlier. Still, he didn't hide the fact that he had no love for Hogan.

SIR ADAM

This has always been strange to us, because without Hogan the business never gets to the level it reached in the '80s. It was more than ten years before the Rock came along. And even his biggest match was against Hogan.

PHANTOM

Many of the old school guys, who had to wrestle sixty minutes a night, have been the most outspoken.

Harley Race: A big, showboaty type, Hogan never took one tenth of the bumps that Flair, myself or people like us have taken.

Ultimately, most of the complaints we heard were about Hogan as a performer. As easy as it would have been to just sit back and line up positive and negative quotes and let the wrestlers tell the whole story, one topic really needed to be addressed. What was he like as a person? For years we'd heard that he was either a wrestler's best friend or worst enemy.

(From a GIR *Radio* Interview)

Sir Adam: *Is Hulk Hogan the best friend a wrestler can have?*

Harley Race: *Ask Brutus "the Barber" Beefcake.*

Sir Adam: *Now that you mention it, it seems like whenever Hogan is hired, Brutus follows, two steps behind.*

Harley Race: *Yep.*

Phantom: *Were you in a position like that? Could you have brought your friends with you back in the day.*

Harley Race: *Sure.*

Phantom: *Did you?*

Harley Race: *Nope.*

Sir Adam: *What's your opinion on that?*

Harley Race: *My opinion? You got a highly inflated ego and you just need "yes people" around you.*

Sir Adam: *Did other wrestlers resent guys who were brought in on someone else's coattails?*

Harley Race: *I'm sure they did. A lot of them deserved to be higher* *than what Brutus Beefcake was. I'm sure there's people that were pissed off.*

PHANTOM

Excellent! Now we have the chance to bash the Beefer too!

SIR ADAM

No, you're missing the point. It's not about bashing anyone. It's about analyzing Hogan's personality, so we can figure out why he's always pulled for certain guys. Was he a nice guy, trying to

Hulk Hogan with his best friend Brutus Beefcake by his side

help out his friends; or was he a conniving star who utilized his power at the expense of others? It's not just Beefcake, but Brian Knobbs, Jimmy Hart and Hacksaw Dugan too. They all benefited from being tight with the Hulkster. Not everyone goes to bat for their friends like that.

PHANTOM

That's true. If I got a job with WWE, I'd instantly forget your name. Actually, I'd trash you so bad you'd never work again.

SIR ADAM

If Vince just gave me an interview, all I would do is trash you. I wouldn't even care about getting the job.

Hulk Hogan (From a 3/03 *GIR Radio* Interview): In the '80s, the tail was wagging the dog. A lot of the main event guys could make a stand.

PHANTOM

When I interviewed Hogan during the WrestleMania 19 press conference in New York City, he recognized the power he wielded during his heyday. In his mind, he was just one of a number of guys who took a stand. But how do his peers see it?

Paul Orndorff: I wouldn't be underneath his skirt like some of his buddies were . . .

George Steele: It's not just Hogan. Don't go there . . . Go back to every champion you ever had in the WWF. Go back to Bruno . . . Every champion knows who he can have the best matches with. They have input.

Sorry George, but we have to go there. We need to find out what made this brother tick, and to do that we have to talk to the guy who, over the years, benefited the most from the Hulkster's generosity. You might know him as Zodiac, Booty Man, Dizzy Hogan, the Disciple, the Barber or even the Butcher. But we know him as . . .

SIR ADAM

The guy with the rusted shears. We couldn't get a hold of Brutus for months. Phone numbers were disconnected, leads went nowhere. Then finally we heard he was appearing at a wrestling convention to be held the day before WrestleMania XX. It was a reunion of some of WrestleMania I's biggest stars . . .

PHANTOM

It was being held in that mecca of wrestling, Carteret, New Jersey . . . So, naturally, we couldn't wait. Unfortunately, Beefcake had recently fallen on hard times, and it was being reported that he was working as a subway token attendant in Boston. Even worse, he had gotten into a little trouble with the law. So we didn't think he was going to show up, let alone talk to us.

SIR ADAM

We had a booth set up at the convention and we scouted the place all day waiting for Brutus' arrival. We were about to head home when in he walked, decked out in his finest Zubaz pants and matching shirt, making small talk with Sensational Sherri and Demolition Axe.

PHANTOM

When I saw him gaze in our direction, I welcomed him with open arms.

SIR ADAM

But all he did was ask us to watch his gym bag. He dropped it right at our feet. All we could see in the bag, which he left wide open, was a large pair of nasty, rusty shears.

PHANTOM

Phantom killing time with SD Jones while Sir Adam tracks down Brutus

They definitely looked like they were left over from his Barber days. If you touched them, you'd definitely need a tetanus shot. I wanted to put on some gloves and hide the bag since I was so pissed that he thought we were his lackeys, but Sir Adam was determined to get the scoop on the Hulkster.

SIR ADAM

As much as I would have loved to have framed David Sammartino for hiding the bag, we couldn't miss this opportunity. So I followed him around the convention, and when SD Jones went to the bathroom, I moved in for the kill. Luckily, Brutus was happy to talk and I got to find out just how lucky Brutus felt to be Hogan's friend all of these years.

Brutus Beefcake: I've known the Hulkster all my life. We're friends. We're brothers from another mother, I mean, closer than brothers. Hulk's the Godfather of my daughter — he's been my best friend since the early '70s. He's done a lot for me. I owe him a lot.

Brutus Beefcake with belt-chain

Beefcake recognizes that he greatly benefited from running with the Hulkster. In fact, he traced Hulk's generosity and kindness back to the very beginning.

Brutus Beefcake: Hogan recruited me. "Come on, you're going to be a wrestler, man." I was scared to death. But all I knew was good things were going to happen when we teamed up.

SIR ADAM

Basically, Hogan told him that he was going to be a wrestler.

PHANTOM

So if Hogan was a lion tamer I guess we'd have bearded women bitching to us now about how Hogan and Beefer got the best pay-offs at Ringling Brothers.

SIR ADAM

Yeah. What if Hogan said, "Brother, we're going to be drag queens?" Would Beefcake have followed him then?

PHANTOM

I don't think so. I didn't follow you when you said the same thing to me . . .

Brutus Beefcake: In WCW I was having problems. "Oh, we can't use Brutus because everybody's going to recognize him. He's Brutus." Hulkster and I put our thinking caps on, stepped back and pondered. Next thing you know, the Disciple popped up on the scene. Nobody knew who he was and the Disciple's overnight deal, brother, was a success — until WCW's poor management forced a lot of people to go. Unfortunately, the Disciple was one of those people.

SIR ADAM

I think I can safely say that everyone knew that Brutus and the Disciple were the same guy. This is getting sad.

Still, rather than being perceived as part of a positive story about two friends making it big in the business, or as part of a friend-ship that withstood the test of time, Beefcake is more often than not part of a punch line.

Sean Waltman: Hulk's very good to his friends. Yeah, sure, having the Booty Man as part as the package . . . Okay, that sucks. Well, put him in the first match.

Matt Borne: When I was wrestling out in Portland, he started out as Dizzy Hogan. I guess he grew up with him or something. He's a good guy, but he's [got] a bit of a goofy side. His work isn't really known to be great.

Jake Roberts: Beefcake is the luckiest human being in the world. Because he was connected with Hogan, for some reason, somehow, for so long, he had a job and he made great money.

SIR ADAM

I've always wondered why Beefcake became a wrestler in the first place. He never seemed to have the in-ring skills of his competitors.

PHANTOM

Sure, his in-ring work left much to be desired. But, you know, he usually got a great crowd response in his WWF days. I think I even enjoyed watching him as a tag team with Greg "the Hammer" Valentine back in the mid '80s.

Chris Kanyon: I was just watching old tapes of Brutus Beefcake and Greg Valentine against the British Bulldogs. Did Brutus deserve to get strung along by Hulk there? I don't know, man. Brutus Beefcake was over. You watch it, maybe he wasn't the greatest worker of all time, but that gimmick was over.

Jake Roberts: Poor Greg Valentine, he was the unluckiest man in the world. He had to do all the Goddamn work in the ring — and get beat too.

SIR ADAM

Just when we'd achieved a positive note — leave it to Jake to burst the bubble.

Brutus Beefcake: I'm just happy to have been there at the top and riding the big wave with the Hulkster all these years. But I just got one more thing to say: it ain't over yet.

SIR ADAM

Sorry, Beefer, but I think it is safe to say it's over.

PHANTOM

After talking with Beefcake, next on our list was the "Mouth of the South," Jimmy Hart. And, man, did Hart love talking about Hogan.

Jimmy Hart: I met Hulk years ago in Memphis when he was just one of the Boulder Brothers. I was in music, doing some stuff with Jerry Lawler. I remember it so vividly, I was in town when one night Terry happened to be in the ring. I think he was in a singles match. He was just a giant back then. I was watching and, I remember, Lawler goes, "What do you think of that guy?" I went, "Oh my God. Man, he's awesome. Look at the people going crazy over him." Lawler goes, "He asked me to manage him. He was gonna give me fifteen percent." And I said, "Are you gonna do it?" And he goes, "Are you crazy? That guy will never make a dime in this business."

SIR ADAM

And Talking . . .

Jimmy Hart: I've seen Hulk go out and do the charities. I've seen him hurt and still make towns because he's really always loved the business. Here's the thing, there's been a lot of people that have been pushed and been able to run with the football. I don't need to mention a lot of them now, but you can sit back and look at all the big names in wrestling who have been given an opportunity. But those people, with the same opportunity, haven't taken it as far as Hulk's taken it. Because they haven't kept their body groomed, they haven't kept themselves in shape, they haven't done other things outside wrestling.

PHANTOM

And right when it was turning into a Hulk Hogan infomercial,

Jimmy Hart riding that Hogan wave of success

Jimmy managed to put into words precisely where Hogan's head was at during his historic run, and why Brutus was allowed to come along for the ride.

Jimmy Hart: When you were Hulk Hogan back then, it was very lonely. You were the main man, you were drawing the money. When we got our booking sheets, we had three towns running most of the time. Everybody looked at it and went, "God, I hope I'm on Hulk's card" — 'cause you knew it was going to sell out. So Hulk would have to come in really, really early, 'cause he was always the last match, and back then Vince didn't have so much security. He was so popular back then, oh my God, wherever he went . . . So I think Brutus was there not only to wrestle, but Vince would have probably paid him just to be with Hulk, to carry his bags, to go to the gym with him, to be there to go work out with him, so he'd have somebody in the limo with him, somebody to eat with. I think that was why he was there. He just happened to be a wrestler. Vince didn't have to pay him just to be a bodyguard or a buddy. I think that's why it was really like that. But we were in some towns where Brutus and Greg had the belts and we made some good money. If he was the drizzling shits, he probably wouldn't have been there.

> One thing that shouldn't be lost in all of this is that it didn't have to be Brutus. Hundreds of others would have lined up for his place. But Hulk was loyal to a long-time friend, helping him achieve the kind of fame and fortune that, based on his wcw run, he would likely never have reached on his own. And as it turns out, there are many more stories about Hogan trying to help other wrestlers — including some that you never would have imagined were in his good graces.

Kamala: I was wrestling Hogan in some big city, it was already sold out, and Hogan wanted me to beat him, but he said not for the belt. Chief Jay Strongbow was the agent at the time. Hulk said, "I just want to let him beat me tonight and the next time we'll come back and we'll still draw a big crowd." Strongbow said, "No, no, no, I don't want him to beat you." So he said, "Come here." Because Hogan kept insisting that I beat him, they went for a little walk down the hall in the building and I kind of followed them. Chief Jay Strongbow told Hogan: "Look, he's just a big black nigger with paint on his face." That's what he told him. Nobody told me he said that, I heard it myself. So, when they finished talking, I went back to the dressing room, and acted like I didn't hear nothing. And when Hogan came back — he didn't know what I'd heard — he said, "Well, I couldn't talk no sense into him. He still wants me to beat you, so you just take most of the match."

Hogan was a real gentleman. He was the one that called me up and asked me about coming to WCW. And I told him, "Yeah, I would love to." I thought I was gonna get a contract. Anyway, Eric Bischoff wouldn't give me a contract, he wouldn't even speak to me. And we had never met before, so I stayed there for about three months. My last match was with Hogan on that Bash at the Beach in 1995. And I got paid for that and that was it.

Ted DiBiase: I had his first match in Madison Square Garden, and he told me that night, "I owe you one buddy." And he never forgot it. When I came back and became the Million Dollar Man, you know, at that time he was in his prime and basically he could decide who he wanted to work with. We had a match. It was an outdoor show somewhere. When that match was over, we got back, I think we were dressing in a trailer, and he looked at me and he winked and said, "It's payback time, pal." That was my cue. He was saying that we would be spending a lot of time in the ring together. When Terry was in his prime, basically, he was the man. And if he liked you it was good.

When the Honky Tonk Man appeared on *Get in the Ring* in 2001, he also spoke of how Hogan could make or break a career. Honky Tonk explained that Hogan was more involved in his run as the longest-reigning Intercontinental Champion of all time than people realize. The title change came about at a time when Vince McMahon was desperate: a new champion had to be crowned after Ricky Steamboat won the belt from Randy Savage at WrestleMania III, because "The Dragon" wanted to take time

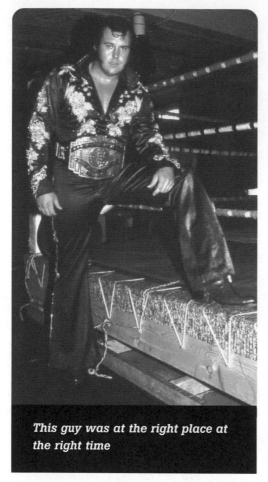

This guy was at the right place at the right time

off to be with his family. McMahon had Butch Reed pegged for the strap, but in Buffalo, New York, on the night he was supposed to take the title, "the Natural" was nowhere to be found.

The Honky Tonk Man (From a 7/01 *GIR Radio* Interview): McMahon wanted the belt in the towns, because we ran a lot of towns. He needed that Intercontinental belt to support main event matches. I just happened to walk by while he and Pat Patterson and Hogan were standing there talking about Butch Reed not being there, and Hogan looked and said, "Put the belt on this guy." And Vince looks around and sees me coming down through there in a white jump suit, looking like Elvis. Baby, he looks at me and says, "That's not a bad idea . . . Come here."

PHANTOM

With all of these stories about Hogan's *positive* influence, we started questioning our years in the wrestling radio business. It was always an accepted fact — handed down from Rich Mancuso to John Arezzi, and then to us, that Hogan was a nightmare behind the scenes.

SIR ADAM

What we learned was that Hogan was humble in the face of most of his '80s contemporaries. Bam Bam Bigelow was right, he should have gone into politics.

Ronnie Garvin: He'll tell you himself, he can't walk on his own without tripping. He told me one time, I was partnered with him once or twice, and he said, "Man, I wish I could work like that."

Bob Orton, Jr.: Hogan, I think, respected me. I'm the guy that he brings up when he was playing in a band and he went outside to the parking lot and he asked a wrestler how to get started. Well, that guy was me. So I think he always treated me fine.

PHANTOM

There's no doubt that he's a captivating guy. Whatever he tells you comes across as larger than life. When I was interviewing him in 2003, he actually had me feeling sorry for him.

Hulk Hogan: I just never could get that breakthrough movie. Somebody out here asked "Stone Cold" if he was jealous of the Rock. Well, I'm jealous. I wish I could've had that breakthrough movie when I was trying to do the action hero thing,

PHANTOM

There I was, feeling bad for a multi-millionaire who could never get that big movie break. While I, on the other hand, had to take the cross-town bus back to my one room apartment. Even as I watched him get into a limo, I still felt sorry for him.

Despite the good things most of the people we spoke to had to say, Hogan still had detractors. These stories have never been reported anywhere else, and illustrate another aspect of Hulk's personality. You're either with him or against him, there is no in-between.

Tony Atlas: Very rarely are you going to get a women to go as far as Hogan went. Wendi Richter almost made it there, but then he got jealous because Wendi Richter was getting a little bit of publicity. And he got her kicked out of the WWF.

Matt Borne: Buzz Sawyer had problems with Hogan back when Hogan was first starting in the business. I guess it was a steroid thing, you know, and Buzz got a bunch of steroids from him and never paid him. Hogan always held that against him. And Buzz beat him up in the dressing room. They fired Buzz because he beat the hell out of Hogan. But anyway, back in those days, if you were in with Hogan, you were in, and if you had problems with Hogan then, you know . . . bye-bye.

PHANTOM

There it was, the back-stabbing Hulkster. The guy who tried to hold people down that weren't named Beefcake or Hart. I knew we were being fooled.

In the mid-'90s, Hogan went from the All-American to the hated leader of the NWO, a heel turn that reinvigorated his career. The NWO Hogan was a vicious character who saw fit to give an extra welcome to David Flair upon his entrance into the business. Whether he intentionally took things too far is up for debate.

David Flair: Hogan said he was gonna hit me a couple of times (with his weightlifting belt). I knew he was gonna hit me, but it was West Virginia, and people got really into it. It was good heat, with the fans and the people at home, and he just kept going at it because the fans were biting. They were throwing batteries and everything in the ring. I think it was kind of a rib on me. You know, you want to wrestle? You want to get in the business? You're getting whipped, like, twenty times.

> It's safe to say that David Flair wasn't a member of the Hogan crew. And neither was Matt Borne. Actually, Borne's negativity is remarkable — he was more heated about the Hulkster than anyone else we spoke with. And, in some ways, it's with good reason.

Matt Borne: Vince wanted Hogan to work with me at WrestleMania IX and Hogan just absolutely refused to work with the clown. That was the original plan, Doink against Hogan. And Hogan wouldn't do it.

> Missing a big WrestleMania main event payday against Hulk Hogan would make anybody bitter. Especially when you consider that Hulk ended up working with his buddy Brutus Beefcake to take on Ted DiBiase and I.R.S. for the tag team championship. Doink wrestled in a preliminary match. But even though Hogan didn't want to work with a Clown, he would with a Mountie . . .

Jacques Rougeau: When he came to the Molson Center, and we were sitting in the dressing room, there were rumors . . . What we may do, what we may not do. Nothing was clear. When we got talking about the finish, the second part of the show was already underway. He came and sat beside me in the dressing room. He said, "Well, what *are* we doing, boss?" He called me boss 'cause it was my show. I looked at him and I was so impressed by him calling me boss. I said, "Well, what are we doing, boss?" So he said, "You know Jacques, let me tell you something. For ten years you've been on the road with me. You know everybody thinks that the main event is the most important match of the evening. But really, the most important match of the evening is the first match — because if you start the people on the right foot, then it's easy to have a good evening. But if you have a shitty match on first, it kind of puts a bad taste in everybody's mouth. Jacques, for all the times that you and your brother have helped me, and now that we're in Montreal, well, you deserve to be a hero here . . . " So what can I say? I know I owe the man.

Hogan went out that night and lost, cleanly, to Jacques Rougeau, Jr. in his hometown.

PHANTOM

I have a tear in my mask.

SIR ADAM

That's beautiful.

PHANTOM

So I guess no more trash talk?

SIR ADAM

No more trash talk.

Buff Bagwell: I partied with him for a lot of years. I've been around him, in a business sense, and from top to bottom I've never seen him be mean to nobody. He's always nice, cordial . . . knew when to switch gears and change outfits and stay cool.

Chris Kanyon: I got to work with Hulk a lot closer than most of these guys that have an opinion . . . I don't think they saw the side of him that I did. I got to work with him on Jay Leno, and it was me, Kidman and Erik Watts training Jay Leno. I got to work with Hogan almost on a daily basis. I think that Hulk loves this business more than anyone.

Diamond Dallas Page: He's loyal to the people that are loyal to him. And in this business there are only a handful of guys that are loyal to each other. It's a different world, man . . .

So not only is Hogan a guy who looks after his friends, he's also not doing anything that other wrestlers wouldn't do.

Sid Vicious: I brought in a few people. I started Harlem Heat in WCW. I brought them in from Texas. I was doing a benefit for Kerry Von Erich's family after his death and I met them there . . . and told them I would try and get them into WCW. It took me awhile, but I got them in. There was a little jealousy, because they were in a main event Pay-per-view their very first month.

Bobby Heenan has known Hulk Hogan since their AWA days and has traveled all over the world with him. And even with all of the criticism of Hogan's in-ring work, and even though Bobby has managed all-time legendary champions like Nick Bockwinkel, Ric Flair and Harley Race, he considers Hogan the sport's greatest of all time.

Bobby Heenan: The greatest worker in the world is Hulk Hogan. He can't arm drag you. He can't head scissors you. He can't do all that. But he can put more asses in the seats than you've ever seen. And that's how I judge a person as a worker. *That* is a worker.

So why is it that so many of his peers love to trash him?

Bobby Heenan: Because none of us really had that much fame. We never walked on the red carpet. We were never on the *Tonight Show*.

SIR ADAM

Turns out, Hulk Hogan is a guy who was just doing what anyone would have done. I don't hate him anymore.

PHANTOM

Me neither. How could you hate the guy who said this to me, during the press conference for WrestleMania 19?

Phantom: Hulk, how many years do you have left?

Hulk Hogan: You know brother, I don't know. Right now, I just take it day-by-day. The business has changed and moved so fast and the guys are so young. Thank God for the loyalty of the fans. I don't plan anything beyond the very next wrestling match, so it's all the luck of the draw at this point. God willing, I'll keep going because I love being around all these people.

SIR ADAM

That was totally irrelevant. You just want to keep rubbing in the fact that I couldn't make that press conference, don't you?

PHANTOM

What happened to the positive ending? You ruined it!

SIR ADAM

You know something, brother? You suck.

Chapter 11

Is Wrestling Fake?

There it is, the dreaded F word. No book on the mysteries of professional wrestling would be complete without it. It's the very word that, when uttered by *20/20*'s John Stossel in 1985, caused "Dr. D" David Shults to slap the reporter silly.

Chris Kanyon: Why fuck up a magician's way of making a living? Stossel didn't ask Dr. D, "Is it fake?" He said: "I think this is fake." Very different. That was historic.

Now, this wasn't any old slap. It really seemed like Dr. D was trying to permanently injure a man who might have been 130 pounds, soaking wet. Stossel later told Barbara Walters that Shults hit him so hard that, "I now have permanent hearing damage."

SIR ADAM

In retrospect, it seems bizarre that *20/20* had to do an investigative piece to find out that wrestling wasn't real.

PHANTOM

I still remember watching it as a kid. Being deathly afraid of Dr. D, but still wanting to know more about pro wrestling.

A young Chris Kanyon was watching as well.

Chris Kanyon: I think the jackass showing how we cut ourselves was worse. I was sixteen years old. The next day, I pulled out a razor and cut my own forehead. A lot of my friends did it too, just to see if it worked.

PHANTOM

That shows you the difference between me and a guy like Kanyon. I had bad dreams about Dr. D boxing my ears, while Kanyon was trying to "get color" like the pros. I guess that's why I ended up talking about wrestling, while he actually got in the ring.

SIR ADAM

I remember cutting my forehead, too. Just to miss school.

PHANTOM

Why didn't you just fake a cold?

SIR ADAM

That's a very good question.

The *20/20* report was one of the first times wrestling's "magician's secrets" were revealed outside the exclusive brotherhood of pros, promoters and insiders. Still, even though the business has long since been exposed, the role of a professional wrestler, once he steps inside the ring, remains essentially the same.

Ronnie Garvin: Politics and wrestling are the same thing. We go into the ring and we entice people to scream and yell and get pissed off. We're playing with emotions. Politicians play with people's emotions, too.

Wrestling fans were probably the only ones who weren't surprised when a veteran wrestler by the name of Jesse "the Body" Ventura managed to convince an entire state that he was Governor material. A grappler's career depends on getting a rise out of an audience — and Jesse was one of the best. In the old days, it was different. Pre-20/20, wrestlers felt the audience had to believe everything they did in the ring — that if it wasn't "real" they wouldn't sell tickets. It was up to the wrestlers to make believers out of the "marks." And it sounds like they had fun doing it.

A casual Larry Zbyszko — just don't ask him about the sleeper hold

Larry Zbyszko: No one believed the sleeper hold really worked. We used to go to shows and have people come into the ring during intermission. We'd make a challenge. We'd put the sleeper hold on you, and if you didn't go to sleep we'd give you 500 bucks. We'd put them to sleep left and right.

Kevin Sullivan: If you could get people to believe in you, then maybe they'd come out again. Our job was to put people in the seats. Our pay depended on it.

They were so convincing that, over the years, many audience members tried to get in on the action.

Ivan Koloff: A knife was thrown at me in the ring. The handle hit me in the back and fell to the mat. Of course, I picked it up and utilized it on my opponent . . . The fan who threw it probably got beat up, because I used it on the good guy.

Today, few fans can imagine ever getting so riled up they'd throw a knife — at anyone besides, say, Triple H. (Just kidding.) Everyone knows its fake . . . right?

Jerry Lynn: It's fixed, not fake.

PHANTOM

Another F word. Fixed . . . like any other All-American sport. Like football, basketball, baseball. With the amount of money involved, they have to be fixed too, right? So why is it always Hulk Hogan that gets a snicker from every smart ass SportsCenter anchor, and not LeBron James?

Rick Steiner: Vince McMahon hurt this business by coming out and spilling his guts about what goes on.

In 1994, in an attempt to avoid government regulation of his business, Vince McMahon admitted that his cash cow was a "work." The results, he conceded, were predetermined. Or, for lack of a better word, *fake*.

PHANTOM

I was shocked when he said it was fake. I always thought
Abdullah the Butcher was really trying to kill people.

SIR ADAM

I always thought some matches — like the championship matches
— were real. Vince broke my heart.

Kevin Sullivan: When I was a kid, I used to go to the matches. And
I'm still a wrestling fan. Out came the Sheik for the first time, the
Original Sheik, and I knew there was something different: I thought,
well, this guy's real. In those days people would say, well, the world
championship matches were real . . .

Chris Kanyon: I think in the back of people's minds, they always
thought it was fake, even back in the '80s. Then it became more
acceptable for wrestlers to talk openly. It's hard to change that.
What, am I going to be the one guy to say, "No, I can't talk like this;
it's real . . ."? I mean, that makes me look stupid. If Vince is out there
telling everybody it's fake, I can't go out and say it's real. To this
day, I still get questioned. It's like, "Do you even read a newspaper?
We told everybody it's fake!"

If that's the case, then why do wrestlers still hate the F word? After
all, it's just a word.

Ted DiBiase: The word fake has negative connotations. You think of
Hollywood, it's a stunt, it's not real, nobody's getting hurt.
Professional wrestling is every bit as physical, if not more physical,
than pro football. There aren't any pads. You take a 300 pound man
and you slam him from six or seven feet in the air — I don't care
what the mat's made of, you're taking a blow.

Reno: Everything you do in the ring is real, only the outcome is pre-determined. You can't fake gravity.

Kevin Von Erich: People say, "Oh, that mat has padding," or "There's a microphone under there." But when you're jumping fifteen feet in the air and coming down on your stomach, I don't care how many layers of carpet are under that canvas, gravity is gravity.

This is like *Sesame Street*. We've finished with the letter F and now we're on to G. Wrestlers point to gravity as the best example of what's "real" about wrestling. Think of the famous Shawn Michaels/Razor Ramon ladder match at WrestleMania X. When Michaels falls off the ladder, he's not faking a fifteen foot, high speed descent. It hurts, and there's no faking pain. And when Mick Foley took multiple unprotected chair shots from the Rock at the 1999 Royal Rumble? It hurt, badly. Chair shots are so painful that "Gorgeous" Jimmy Garvin winces just thinking about them.

Jimmy Garvin: How do you pull a chair?

SIR ADAM

These guys are professionals, they know what they are doing in the ring. But the average fan doesn't appreciate how much pain is involved in nearly every single maneuver. By using the word "fake," it sounds like anyone could work a match. Let me tell you, from personal experience, you can't.

PHANTOM

In 1996, Sir Adam and I were invited to the Wild Samoan training school in Allentown, Pennsylvania. On the phone, Afa said, "You guys will have some fun." I thought I'd throw on the old mask and singlet and get ready to roll around the ring a little, maybe even throw some patented Phantom arm bars. But there was nothing fun about that day.

SIR ADAM

It seemed like the only guy having a good time was Afa. He laughed as our bodies broke down before his eyes. Not only were there no Phantom armbars, there were no Phantomsaults, no Sir Adam bombs, no nothing.

PHANTOM

I thought it would be no big deal, but I couldn't have been more wrong. In fact, my body was done after fifteen Hindu Squats. A Hindu squat is where you stand in place and bend your knees, going up and down. When we finally moved on to push ups, leg lifts and stretching, my body was giving me signals I'd never felt before. After taking fifty back bumps, Afa said I still needed more work. I cried and called it a day.

Vic Grimes: It's all about being trained to learn how to fall. You're as good as you can bump.

SIR ADAM

When I saw Phantom curled into a ball by the ring post I couldn't help thinking how lucky he was. I prayed for the back bumps to end. I soon found out front bumps were worse. Although I always knew it wasn't a trampoline in there, I will never forget how hard the mat really is. I remember thinking: Just hold on until we started learning moves . . . Then, when Afa said we were going to run five miles first, I threw up and called it a day.

PHANTOM

Falling on your back sounds easy, but it isn't. If you don't fall the right way, it hurts. A lot. And I couldn't do it properly. For two weeks, I really couldn't walk. Okay, I walked, but I looked like

The phenomenal A.J. Styles mid-flight

Redd Foxx in *Sanford and Son.* I waddled in pain. And we're not talking clotheslines, leapfrogs or chair shots — a few back bumps and Hindu Squats were enough to make me realize that wrestling was far from fake.

AJ Styles: To say its fake is ridiculous. I played football in high school and I wrestled in high school. I've been hurt more in professional wrestling than in any other sport I have ever played.

Every wrestler we've interviewed agrees that the ring is a dangerous place. You can be seriously hurt, even if you know what you're doing. And there's always a significant amount of pain involved. One big problem the pros face is that there is no off-season. In other sports, athletes have at least a couple of months off — time for their bodies to heal. In wrestling, you work, pack up your stuff, move on to the next town, and do it all over again.

Chris Candido: You get some kind of an injury every single time you go in there.

Every night, on every card, there are numerous wrestlers working through severe pain — the type of agony an ordinary person can't even imagine. If they want to make money, they can't just call in sick.

SIR ADAM

I couldn't even hold a fork after my Wild Samoan experience. Let alone do a triple moonsault off the top rope.

Bobby Eaton: You learn to deal with it.

Actually, for most wrestlers, pain becomes a normal part of life.

Hacksaw Duggan: You gotta be able to play with pain. If you tear a hamstring or something you tape it up and get back in the ring.

Jimmy Valiant: Years ago brother, we never quit. No matter what injuries you had, you'd just tape up, man, and keep going.

Ronnie Garvin: I burned my foot on a motorcycle once, and I had a third degree burn. My foot swelled up twice its normal size. I could hardly walk. I showed up at the matches and I put my foot in my boot, but I couldn't lace it, so I taped it. It was about three inches away from me being able to lace it that's how swollen it was and I went to the ring and wrestled.

SIR ADAM

What kind of tape do wrestlers use? It's so good it can hold body parts together? Some company is really missing the marketing boat here.

PHANTOM

A company that makes wrestler-strength tape is one I'd invest in.

The good old days: everyone taped up and hobbling. But that was then, right? Amazingly enough, the guys today have the same mentality.

AJ Styles: I broke my foot. It was the four-way elimination match for the X division title when TNA first started. My foot was broken, but I wasn't gonna tell anybody. I wasn't gonna lose my spot.

Eddie Guerrero (From an 11/01 *GIR Radio* Interview)**:** I don't have an ulnar collateral ligament now in my left arm. All I do, I guess, is cheat a little bit more to the right side . . .

Erik Watts: I remember times when I couldn't get out of bed, but still had to be at the next town to wrestle. No matter how bad you hurt, if you don't produce, you don't get paid. There's so few spots, for so many people, you're not going to take the chance of not showing up.

It's the same today as it's always been: wrestlers know there will always be someone ready, willing and able to take their place. Still, there's a difference between working with pain and actually enjoying it. And what we found out is that there have been a select few in the sport that actually love the pain. The late Johnny Valentine is someone most veterans point to as the perfect example of a wrestler who thrived on the pain.

Ronnie Garvin: A guy who likes it? Johnny Valentine. You'd hit him and he'd look at you, and you'd have goose bumps and he'd say, "Harder."

Jimmy Valiant: You hit Johnny Valentine, man, and no matter how hard you hit him he just laughs.

Of course, today, some legendary ECW performers come to mind.

Erik Watts: Some of the new guys like pain, it seems. Like Balls Mahoney. Sandman — it seems like he really gets off on it. And it doesn't seem like Sabu really minds it . . . You know, of all people, I think Mick Foley would tell you something different. It's not that he loves pain, it's just that he'll do anything to freak the audience out. Therefore, in order to do that, the level of moves he does, you're gonna have pain.

Buff Bagwell: Perry Saturn and Sabu. Every single night they went out and did the most unbelievable stuff. My God, I thought, are they getting off on the pain?

PHANTOM

Hey, this is my book. No one mentions Perry Saturn's name again.

Sabu, perhaps more than any other contemporary wrestler, is the guy whose pain threshold leaves others mystified.

Chris Candido: If he doesn't enjoy pain . . . I mean, he should have been in a wheelchair years ago.

Reno: Sabu? He's a sick bastard . . .

PHANTOM

Most performers believe it comes with the territory. I think they all love it, they get off on hurting and bleeding and getting stitches.

Bobby Heenan: Are you stupid?

Tommy Young: If you love pain, there's got to be something wrong with you.

Okay, Sabu is the exception and not the rule.

PHANTOM

All right, I can take Bobby Heenan, former wrestler and manager, calling me an idiot. But, come on, Tommy Young? He was just a referee, what does he know about pain?

Referee Tommy Young: The match was between Mike Rotunda and "Wildfire" Tommy Rich. Tommy was supposed to do something that wasn't even part of the actual finish . . . He was supposed to simply shove me in the back . . . I wasn't even supposed to take a bump. Trouble was, when he did it he lifted his leg up and tripped me and the ropes were close by. I tried to grab them, but missed. I took the ropes between my eyes, my neck snapped back, and for about a minute I was Christopher Reeve. The feeling came back, but I was all screwed up. I had to have an operation, and they had to remove the vertebrae. I always knew that I might get hurt because of my style — it was kind of reckless — but I never dreamed I would be injured like that.

> Unfortunately, everyone who steps inside the ring runs the risk of suffering a serious, debilitating injury — one they may never come back from.

Jeff Hardy (From a 3/03 *GIR Radio* Interview)**:** I've been concerned about it, especially after Droz, 'cause he was just a big jacked-up dude that was so healthy. And with the blink of an eye it can all change. I've always been aware of that. I'm still so nervous before every match and I think that the biggest reason is that I'm aware that there's a chance I might not be walking after. I don't care how big of a match it is or how small. It can happen at any time. I'm trying not to hesitate when I jump off ladders.

> Of course, injuries can happen at any time — not just when you're jumping off a ladder. Rob Van Dam broke his leg doing a fairly routine (for him at least) baseball slide. Even the simplest move, one that you've performed in every match of your career, can be your last.

Paul Orndorff: I went to pick up Mark Jindrak for a piledriver. He was young, and it could've been either me or him getting hurt. In the position I had him in, it could've been bad. It was just one of these things. I mean, if you ever look at the film, it was just a positioning thing. I just whipped my neck back. My back . . . it's gone. I cannot sit for a long period of time, or stand. And some days it's like a toothache — it just throbs.

Just that quickly, Mr. Wonderful was not so wonderful anymore. So, wrestlers do what they can to protect one another, but sometimes it isn't enough.

Justin Credible: We're conditioned to go out there and not necessarily kill each other, to protect each other. Night in, night out, we have to work with the same people.

Justin Credible wincing in pain

Sean Waltman: When I was nineteen, wrestling Bill Wilcox, he climbs up to the top rope. I'm on the floor, and there's no pads on the floor. He dives off the top, and goes sailing over my head. So, I jumped up and caught him. All his weight came down on my head and I landed on the cement. I was knocked out cold, and had a blood clot on my brain.

A brain injury was Waltman's reward for following the unwritten rule: always protect your opponent. But this isn't the end of Sean's story. He's had another serious, life-altering injury.

Sean Waltman: I was working with Lex Luger at a Minnesota house show and he shot me in the ropes and gave me a big belly boost in the air. I was supposed to land on my stomach. And he shot me up so high, I came straight down on my head. I knew something was terribly wrong, because my whole left side started atrophying. I was in excruciating pain. My fifth vertebrae was completely fractured and there was almost a chunk of it hanging off.

And to top it off . . .

Sean Waltman: I've probably had a dozen concussions.

Is Sean just an injury prone wrestler with incredible stories? No, the scary thing is, they all talk this way. You're an oddball if you've never suffered an injury.

Viscera: I've had a broken hand, a cracked sternum, I've been relatively lucky.

Imagine, you've had a cracked sternum — one of the most painful injuries a human being can endure — and you consider yourself lucky?

SIR ADAM

I'm still telling stories about the time I had that double ear infection.

Jacques Rougeau: Brian Blair leapfrogs . . . I start running. And as he side-stepped me — I don't know how he did it — he lost his balance. And instead of just giving me a working punch in the back of the shoulders, he gave me a slamming clothesline which put me off balance. So my face hit the second rope instead of going through the second and third. I needed forty-some stitches — it tore up my whole face. They had a plastic surgeon come in and redo my face.

Erik Watts: It was a battle royal, and I remember it was Mark Canterbury and Tex Slazenger. I was above their heads, like in a press slam. Someone backed up and got punched, sold the punch, hit those two guys and those two guys lost control and threw me over the ropes to the floor. I had blood in my nose and in my mouth, but I was so happy, elated, that I could move, that it was kind of weird. I kind of jumped up, acting like nothing happened, you know? And then I had to start re-selling it, because I was just so freaked. You know, when you fall that far and you hit and you hear you hear your body splat it's like: Oh yeah, I gotta be dead.

It wasn't until about six or seven months later that my wife, she kind of saved my life. I was choking on some blood that came up at night. She kicked me out of bed and cleared my airway and said, "What in the world's that?" I said, "I don't know, I've been bleeding a little bit after matches." And then when they went and checked it — there was a tear in my esophagus. The only bad thing about it is, when they fixed it, they did kind of like a hernia type surgery to keep some of the acid away from the lining. They stitched a wire mesh around my esophagus. So, to this day, that's why I'll probably never be at the weight I was in the WWF because I choke on most every meal I eat. It's hard for me to eat in public. I don't eat around too many people, because I never know if my esophagus is spasming. You don't know until you swallow. And once you swallow, it's too late. You fight to try and make it go down, and you're begging it to come up. It gets kind of exciting every once in a while.

Ken Shamrock: I tore my lung, and I almost died. I was getting powerbombed by Vader. He powerbombed me once, and I already had a bad rib. He powerbombed me again and my lungs filled up with blood. I was coughing it out. He wanted to powerbomb me again, but I said, "No way." I went to the doctors and they said, "Good thing." Because my lung would have torn completely and filled up with blood and I would have drowned.

> Live, on *Nitro*, Rick Steiner went for an off-the-top-rope bulldog on Buff Bagwell. Something went wrong. Bagwell was paralyzed, laying in the ring for almost thirty minutes.

Buff Bagwell: That was the worst thing that ever happened to me in my life. I was just laying there. It was like: "You're paralyzed; you're done." That's how real it was. If you watch the tape, it's unbelievable. My arms are flopping, I can't hold anything up. You can imagine what's going through your head.

Bagwell eventually recovered and went on to piss off just about everyone ever involved with the wrestling business. Now, years later, does either man involved know exactly what went wrong?

Buff Bagwell: I've taken that move a billion times. I guess he kind of missed me. I tried to catch up to him — and *wham!*

Rick Steiner: Looking back, I can't really tell what went wrong. It was just one of those freak things. It looked like he tucked his head too much and jammed his neck, but I don't know. Freak accidents happen all the time.

They certainly do. Just ask Alan Funk, AKA Kwee-wee, AKA "Mr. I got really messed up when I was wrestling in Helsinki, Finland."

Alan Funk: Mike Sanders was my partner and we were wrestling Elix Skipper and Sonny Siaki. I did a couple of spots with Elix then he tagged Sonny in. Sonny went for a split-legged moonsault off the corner and his knees smashed my face. I actually had a skull fracture, so I was bleeding out of my ears — like somebody was pouring a pitcher of blood out of my ears. It didn't really feel that bad at the point of impact, but I knew it was bad because I couldn't see and blood was pouring out of my ears. I'm like: "Shit, that ain't good." You train for that stuff all your life and you never expect something like that to happen. I think the crowd thought it was just part of the act or something. I had total face reconstruction. I got five plates in my face and a bunch of screws. My eyeballs were out of my head, my nose was on the left side of my face. They had to reconstruct my whole face. The doctor told Mike Sanders that I probably wasn't gonna make it through the night.

Scary stuff — as far from fake as things get. And Alan Funk isn't coming back; he's on the permanently injured list. But what about Sonny Siaki, the man who caused the horrific injury?

Alan Funk: I got pissed off at Sonny. He never did come to the hospital to see me.

How could you be so cruel, not even visiting a guy you almost killed?

Lodi: One of the things I learned? When someone suffers a serious injury and is going to be out for a long time: all your friends make that one customary visit or that one customary call. It's like, "Hey, man, I hope you get better." Then everybody disappears.

Lance Storm demonstrating why Randy Orton needed two major shoulder surgeries by the age of 25

I don't think anybody wants to end up in that situation, seeing you with a neck brace. They're reminded: "That could be me."

In an effort to deal with the harsh realities of injuries and the stress they cause, some wrestlers begin to abuse medication.

Chris Candido: We take pain medication; we get hurt more, we take more. No one's going to write you a prescription . . . So, you try to buy more . . . And as is evident in the numerous guys that we've lost the last couple of years, you get hooked on it . . . And I did too.

The mainstream media uses stories like Candido's to make all wrestlers seem like drug addicts. You've read about it in newspapers and magazines; it's all over the media: "They all do lots and lots of pills." Yes, some guys do self-medicate. But what happens when people outside the media buy into this wholesale? Well, it almost cost Chris Kanyon his life.

Chris Kanyon: Literally, we were wrestling in a barn — I'm not kidding. It was a state fair and where we dressed was actually a barnyard. Cowshit on the floors and stuff. And when I got thrown out of the ring I landed on my shoulder and cut it open. It got infected. It got worse and worse, and when I had it x-rayed, because the infection was so bad, the swelling had pushed the bone out of the socket. They diagnosed it as a dislocated shoulder. But it wasn't dislocated, it was pushed out of the socket because the swelling was so bad. So I went home, and the next day I had an MRI. It was a Saturday morning and I passed out. I was sleeping pretty much till Sunday night. My friends rushed me to the hospital. Next thing I remember was waking up on Monday night. The doctor said, "We've got to operate on your shoulder." They did that and two days later I was still in the hospital. When I woke up I couldn't breathe. Basically, my lungs filled up with fluid. Usually your blood oxygen content should be 96–98 percent. When it gets down to 90, they freak. Mine went down to 46. The doctors pretty much thought I was going to die and they were slapping me in the face saying I had to stay awake. I asked them the next day how it happened, because I was afraid it would happen again, and they said I had an allergic reaction to the morphine. They told me that they assumed, because I was a pro-wrestler, I'd probably experienced drug use. So they allowed me to do more morphine than they probably should have . . . And I'm one of the rare guys — you can ask anyone — I never did the pills, never really partied.

So, the next time you hear someone say that wrestling is fake, use this information and stand up for our dear old sport. These stories prove it! With what these athletes go through, it just can't be fake.
So, if it isn't fake, then what is it?

Paul Orndorff: It's an art . . .

Chapter 12

Is There Life After Wrestling?

Bobby Heenan: Unless you've been in it, you don't understand what walking away means. You never walk away.

Retirement. It's a word that brings a smile to most people's faces. Thoughts of warm weather, early-bird dinners and endless rounds of golf are enough to make most men look forward to the day when they can call it a career. In wrestling, that's just not the way it works. Most grapplers either can't leave, refuse to leave, or are taken out kicking and screaming.

Today, "Nature Boy" Ric Flair is still styling and profiling at the tender age of fifty-five. Abdullah the Butcher is still slicing people's foreheads well past his sixty-seventh birthday and Terry Funk, believed to be more than eight thousand years old, still performs gravity-defying moonsaults. There is no disputing that Abdullah, Ric and Terry are "first ballot" Hall of Famers. They've made a lot of money during their careers and reached the very top of their profession. So, why do they continue to put their bodies on the line when many people their age are grateful they can go for a walk without needing to take a nap afterwards?

(From a May 2002 *GIR Radio* Interview with Abdullah the Butcher):

Phantom: Do you see yourself ever retiring? Hanging up those boots and putting away the fork?

Abdullah: I'll never retire. It's in my blood. That's it. You can't stop.

Phantom: It's just in your blood?

Abdullah: That's it. Number one, I don't need nothing. The main part is I like to step in the ring. I like to do what I do and I'm still doing it. A lot of the fans come up to me and say, "We've been watching you for a long time." And they're still coming out to see me.

Don't get on this guy's bad side

We normally wouldn't argue with a guy who gets his kicks stabbing people with kitchen utensils, but it isn't that simple. Our research revealed that for most wrestlers, the sport is like an addiction. They couldn't leave it behind if they tried, and most of them don't want to. Jimmy "Boogie Woogie Man" Valiant is celebrating over forty years in wrestling.

Jimmy Valiant: Walk away? Walk away from what? This is my whole life. This is all I've ever done, all I've ever wanted to do.

SIR ADAM

In the '80s, I remember thinking that Jimmy Valiant was the oldest-looking person I had ever seen. I can't believe he's still going today. Actually, I can't believe I used to run around my house singing "The Boy from New York City," putting my sisters in sleeper holds and pretending I was Jimmy Valiant.

PHANTOM

And I'm the weird one?

Jimmy touches on a little-discussed fact. For many wrestlers, the sport becomes the core of their very existence. You're not going to find a Jimmy Valiant playing tennis or gardening in his spare time. He's a wrestler, and will be until the day he dies.

Jake Roberts: I think the guys that walk away never loved it. Truly. Because to me it's insane to think that you could give up the love. It would be like saying, "Okay, I don't love my mom anymore." It's always been about the love of the game for me, man. Life after wrestling? I don't think that's possible. I don't think I'll ever quit.

It isn't the money that fuels a guy like Jake. While Jake's family and personal problems have been well-documented, his passion for professional wrestling is unbridled and his relationship with the business is one he has always cherished.

Jake Roberts: It's definitely not the lifestyle. It's definitely not the travel. It's definitely not the promoters. It's the ability to masturbate people's emotions, to take them on a ride they can't get anywhere else. When you can put one or a hundred or a thousand people in the palm of your hand, and make them either love you or hate you, want to put you on their shoulders and carry you out and take you home with them, or kill you in a matter of moments — my friend, that's an unbelievable thrill. And when you can look at a child and he's happy and smiling and you see a sparkle in his eye, that's great. When you look at the grandmother ready to stab you with a damn pen knife 'cause she's pissed at you, you got to love it. There's nothing fun about getting on an airplane every day and traveling. The only time I truly enjoyed it was when the damn bell rang. Do you think it's fun sitting in a locker room looking at a somebody's nuts for five hours?

PHANTOM

Considering that his contemporaries included King Kong Bundy, Kamala, and Uncle Elmer, Jake must have *really* loved the sport.

SIR ADAM

So, you think it would have been better for Jake to have to look at the nuts of a skinny guy like Sam Houston?

PHANTOM

First of all, that's his half-brother. Secondly, do you have to resort to your patented nut jokes? You've been so good until now.

Like Jake, many wrestlers accept that they'll be a part of the business until they die. And overall, they don't try to fight it.

Bobby Eaton: I'll probably never be out of it completely. Everybody says they're gonna retire, but I just watched a show last week and they said Terry Funk's coming back out of retirement for the hundredth time. It's in my blood, I guess.

Chris Candido: Why stop? I look at Terry Funk. I worked with Terry Funk a couple of months ago and the man just beats you to death. And Gypsy Joe, I wrestled him in 1990, and he said, "Chop me." And I'm looking at the guy, and he's a million years old, and I want to have respect for him, so I gave him kind of a light chop, not a pussy chop, but he turned me around and beat the hell out of me. If they can still go, then I have no excuse.

Chris is right. Just listen to Terry talking about a match he had a few years ago, in Japan, against Mr. Pogo. Keep in mind that at the time Terry was 52. After the match, Pogo was never the same again.

(From an 8/96 *GIR Radio* Interview with Terry Funk):

Terry Funk: *Barbed wire around the ring on two sides, then they have glass on the other two sides. If you had the ring North, South, East and West, the East and West side would have barbed wire. The North and South wouldn't have ropes, but glass. And then, below the glass, they have bombs and barbed wire. So — a very dangerous match. I was very, very lucky that Pogo went into the bombs first,* because he didn't come back. I had an easy night. I really did. It lasted about seven minutes, I almost felt guilty taking my pay.

Terry Funk showing how close he was to getting "blown up" in Japan

Phantom: *We heard he broke his kneecap and retired.*

Terry Funk: *I don't know what happened, but when I left he was still in the hospital. I know he was injured in the explosion. Gosh, those things are quite dangerous. I've been real fortunate over there.*

Phantom: *What keeps you going?*

Terry Funk: I really enjoy wrestling in front of people and giving them my best, whether that sounds stupid or not — trying to give them their money's worth. I love the business. I don't care if I get blown up.

Of course, not everyone can defy both the odds and time like a Terry Funk or Gypsy Joe. But even grapplers whose age prevents them from competing still find a way to stay involved.

Pez Whatley: For me there hasn't been an "after," there's been a slow down. There hasn't been an "after wrestling" because I try to stay in touch by training some young kids, having little shows every now and then, and just associating with other wrestlers.

Jimmy Valiant: I have a wrestling camp and a hall of fame museum. Something I give back to the wrestling fans. They can come any Sunday from 12 to 4 o'clock and be my guest, spend the day with me. It don't cost nothing, not a dime to get in. You just come and watch my kids train. We have matches and you can enjoy the hall of fame museum.

Jake Roberts: I'm training students. That way, when I'm eighty years old and in a rest home, and I pinch a nurse on the ass and they tie me to the bed, at least I can watch guys who know what the hell they are doing.

To this day, Ric Flair still entertains fans like few before him — and like few will ever do once he actually retires. At this point we won't even bother to get into how WWE would not let us interview Flair. We were able to speak with Ric's former manager, Bobby Heenan, however. And "The Brain" gave us his take on Ric's longevity.

Bobby Heenan: Ric is in his fifties, yet he is still a valuable commodity. Ric Flair will always be something. I watched a thing on TV the other day, the guy from American Idol, Randy Jackson, was saying "I could go to a Black church every week and find fifty-two of the greatest singers you're ever gonna find, but I can't find a whole bunch of stars." Ric Flair is a star. Anybody can grow their hair long; anybody can buy a can of 99 bleach and do their hair. Anybody can buy a robe. And everybody can say, "Whoo!" But there's only one Ric Flair.

While many view Ric's ability to compete at fifty-five as a tribute to his longevity, others see it as staying past his prime. While no one questions his place in wrestling history, some critics think it's crazy that he gets in the ring as often as he does. That in doing so, he tarnishes his legendary status.

(From a *GIR Radio* Interview with Ronnie Garvin):

Sir Adam: Ric Flair still wrestles and he's in his fifties. What you would you say to him today?

Ronnie Garvin: Well, I don't know, I never tell people what to do, but to me it's embarrassing. I mean, we all look at life differently. Maybe he needs the money, I don't know the situation. You know, I just didn't want to be in the ring when I was forty-five. I was in good shape, not too many injuries . . . I felt good and I just said, "It's time." I just walked away from it. You see it in a lot sports. You're fifty, and you're a senior citizen. You should be out of the business. Senior citizens don't belong in a ring.

(From a *GIR Radio* Interview with Harley Race):

Harley Race: Last time I saw him wrestle in St. Louis, I said, "Ricky, my God, why haven't you retired? You know you've had one of the better careers and as far as the wrestling part of it, you're destroying it."

Phantom: So you think he's ruining the illusion in a way?

Harley Race: He's ruining the Ric Flair image, sure.

One of GIR's favorite guests, Sid Vicious

Sir Adam: Do you think he still does it for the money, or does he just love wrestling and can't give it up?

Harley Race: You just said it, he loves the limelight.

SIR ADAM

I think Ric Flair has meant so much to wrestling that even if he is 1/100th of what he once was, it will not ruin his image with long-time fans. In fact, he's more entertaining today than most younger wrestlers. However, I do worry that younger fans won't watch the old videos and understand just how good Ric was in his heyday.

Luckily, Ric's body has held up — he can decide for himself whether or not he still wants to wrestle. Others aren't so lucky. Sid Vicious is one of those wrestlers. In 2001, a horrifically broken leg put an end (at least for now) to his full-time career. Love him or hate him, you can't deny that Sid's headlined all over the world. He's even been a main event performer at several WrestleManias. To say that he didn't go out the way he wanted to is an understatement.

Sid Vicious: I don't think any idiot in the world would say they'd want to end their career with a compound fracture. With having to learn how to walk and run all over again at the age of forty. No, I didn't want it to end like that. I did have a vision of how I wanted it to end. There were two companies when I was considering this: I've got a year, two years, left; let's do some serious business. I had written out a couple different scenarios and I put different names in different places on it. Of course, anything is changeable, but believe it or not, I had it all written out . . . just waiting for the right time. And then, of course, I broke my leg.

> Sid is still rehabbing, still hoping one day make a comeback. The hardest thing for him to deal with has not been the actual pain, but the fact that he won't get to go out on his own terms.

Sid Vicious: If I could have walked away like I planned, I could sleep real easy. But I go to sleep every night thinking that I'm gonna fix all this and one day get to do exactly what I hoped to do. But now I don't know if it's possible.

SIR ADAM

> This is the perfect example of why we haven't succeeded in the wrestling radio business: our show is cursed. A few years back, Sid was one of the biggest names in the sport and a frequent guest on our program. Sid always took the time to return our phone calls and was one of the best guests we ever had, both because he has a unique insight and because he's brutally honest. So what happens? He breaks his leg. And we're left asking Rusty Brooks what it's like to lose nearly every match of your career.

PHANTOM

> It never fails, the *Get in the Ring Radio* curse always strikes. Ernest Miller, a great friend of the show, was on a bunch of times; we had a great rapport. When he got hired by WWE we were so happy — we had an "in." Three days later word got out: Vince McMahon banned his employees from talking to "wrestling media outlets."

Some wrestlers have been forced out for other reasons. The business has changed so much over the last five years, and there simply aren't enough spots available. Rick Cornell, better known as Reno in wcw, was just getting his career off the ground when the company folded. Although his contract was initially picked up by wwe, he was soon released. When wwe's roster was merged with wcw's, superstars like Booker T and Diamond Dallas Page were spared the axe, but there was little room for relatively unproven talent. Just a few years earlier, television ratings and live attendance were at an all time high, and wrestling seemed like a great career choice. With the blink of an eye, it was over.

Reno: I miss it tremendously because it's my passion, it's what I love doing. I loved being in that ring, I loved entertaining people, I loved the athleticism. It's a shame to see the empire come to an end. Because if it didn't, I would still be wrestling.

Many performers became casualties of the merger. Today, they're forced to find other means of income.

Chris Kanyon: At this stage of my life, my career — I'm thirty-four years old — I've got to start thinking of how I'm going to pay the bills four, five, six years from now. And how I'm going to start planning for my retirement.

Alan Funk: It sucks, but unfortunately the business took a turn for the worse. It's like if half of the NFL teams, all of a sudden, just up and quit. Where the hell is everybody gonna go? At a certain point you gotta think about something else. There's not enough spots for everybody in the business.

Joanie "Chyna" Laurer: These guys have dedicated their lives to the profession of wrestling . . . But when there's a monopoly, what are you going to do?

PHANTOM

I'm getting depressed. Let's talk about some of the positives, like not being on the road . . .

There are certain things about the business that former wrestlers don't miss. Like the unbelievable travel schedule the career demands. While most of us look forward to, and spend a great deal of money on trips to another part of the world, almost everyone in wrestling agrees that the road is one of the most grueling parts of the job. It's a never-ending odyssey that has them driving hundreds of miles to get from town to town, and flying across the world and back for overseas tours — all of which leaves them with little time to do anything but wrestle, eat, work out and sleep. So, despite being in a different town three, four or even five nights a week, most wrestlers don't do a whole lot of sightseeing.

Sid Vicious: When I was on the road and I worked out twice a day, I didn't have the opportunity to see anything. I didn't get to see any of the scenery. I wanted to take advantage of the last year or so. Take some pictures. But I never did. And of course, being on last every night, I was the last one in the building.

Kevin Sullivan: When you travel as a wrestler, unless you really go out of the way and squeeze some time in or go before an event, which is very hard to do, all you really see is the airport, the arena, the hotel bar and the hotel.

PHANTOM

If you've never seen a group of wrestlers at a hotel bar you *must* put that on your list of things to do. You can read all the newsletters, magazines and websites you want, but seeing Greg "the Hammer" Valentine walking around a bar holding three beers at a time is something I'll never forget.

Despite traveling throughout Asia, Europe and North America during his lengthy career, finally, at the age of fifty-five, Kevin Sullivan feels that he's getting to see the world for the first time.

Kevin Sullivan: Now, when I travel, I travel for pleasure. We go to Europe twice a year. We're going to Salt Lake City to go skiing for four days. I went to New York City for Christmas.

PHANTOM

What a bunch of babies. For years, I used to commute an hour from New York City to do the radio show. How much worse can it get, sitting on a dirty commuter train?

Bobby Heenan: I've been on the road since 1965. Every day, every week, I had someplace I had to be. I had to go by airline flight numbers — I had to land at a certain time, I had to get my car at a certain time, I had to find a hotel, I had to go get a hotel, check into my room, had to go upstairs. A lot of guys go to the gym; I take a nap. Then you get a towel, put it in your bag, change clothes, go downstairs, try to find the building. You find the building, you try to park your car so the hillbillies don't cut your tires. Then you go inside the building, you do your performance — then you come out and you go back to the hotel. You go to the bar, you have two to sixty beers, and then you go upstairs to bed. You get up at five in the morning, you pack your bag again, you go downstairs, you try to find out where the return parking lot is for the rental car and then you go stand in line at the airport. Then you start all over again. And that's just about what it is.

It's safe to say that Bobby doesn't miss the road.

Bobby Heenan: It's like missing the clap. I mean, what it took to get there was great, but I don't want the aftereffects.